Florence Bell

Alan's Wife

A dramatic study in three scenes

Florence Bell

Alan's Wife
A dramatic study in three scenes

ISBN/EAN: 9783337307714

Printed in Europe, USA, Canada, Australia, Japan

Cover: Foto ©Thomas Meinert / pixelio.de

More available books at **www.hansebooks.com**

ALAN'S WIFE. A DRA-MATIC STUDY IN THREE SCENES. FIRST ACTED AT THE INDE-PENDENT THEATRE IN LONDON.

With an Introduction by
WILLIAM ARCHER.

LONDON: HENRY AND CO.
BOUVERIE STREET, E.C. 1893.

The
Editor's Preface.

I T may be interesting to recount here the history of how I came to accept the play entitled *Alan's Wife*. Miss Robins, in the earlier days of the Independent Theatre, promised me very kindly that she would act for me some time or other; and many months after, she incidentally mentioned that she had a play with her which she would like me to hear. She spoke with great enthusiasm about it, and I, eager to obtain a play by an English author, begged her to lose no time, and to appoint at once a day for reading. I came, and Miss Robins read *Alan's Wife* to me. I shall never forget the impression it made upon me. The first Act, with its glorious sunshine, its idyllic picture of woman's love and woman's admiration for the physical beauty of her husband, charmed me; and when Miss Robins, in her exquisite delivery, came to the sad end of this Act, which cast a gloom on the bright and joyful atmosphere, I was so eager to hear the rest that I would barely grant her time to pause. And the deeper grew the gloom of the action the more did it thrill me. Here was a drama, a slice of human life, as Jean Jullien has it, put upon the stage with

art, and yet so naturally that it made my heart quiver within me. When it was over, and Miss Robins had read the last speech, it seemed to me like one immense outburst of an agonising soul; I was speechless and overcome. I had not heard a play,—I had lived it, and suffered with the wretched heroine. All I could say was: "We shall do that play; we will produce it as soon as we can. It is a beautiful tragedy." And then I rushed away, and finished my evening in a Music Hall, for my head and my heart were full, and unfit for serious work; I wanted something to divert my thoughts. It was an unforgetable evening, and each time I was present at the rehearsals, imperfect as they necessarily were in the beginning, I experienced the same feeling. *Alan's Wife* never failed to draw a tear from me.

After the production, when war raged about the play, when the *pros* and *cons* stood fiercely opposed to one another, when in the judgment there was no compromise, when it was either mercilessly condemned or highly praised,—afterwards, when I had read every opinion, and was called upon to express my own in *The Westminster Review*, I wrote as follows :—

"Undoubtedly, after *A Woman of no Importance*, the production of *Alan's Wife* was the most exciting event in the theatrical world in April. For a long time no play has elicited so much comment, such high praise, and such virulent abuse, as this psychological and physical study of a woman's character. This, in itself, proves, we think, that the work is one of more than ordinary merit. We will not dive into the question whether those who have condemned the play have done so rightly; but this we cannot refrain from stating, that it is a great shame that in certain newspapers every play produced at the Independent Theatre is howled down and stigmatised as abominable. It is unworthy that men who rule over large mouthpieces of public opinion should allow such prejudice, such absolute dishonesty, for the simple reason that the Independent Theatre endeavours to cut new paths.

"What we admire so greatly in *Alan's Wife* is the utter simplicity, the wonderful mixture of light and shade with which the author has brought his picture on the canvas. In the first Act it is all light and love and glory, and revelling in the expected joy of Jean's approaching motherhood. A flood of sunshine glides over the stage; then clouds gather, and suddenly all the brightness, all the happiness disappear : Jean's husband, Alan, is brought home, a victim to his duty. The child is born a cripple : Alan's death fathered the misfortune of the unborn child. Its mother, who adores strength and vigour as a divinity, loudly accuses herself that she has brought such a being into the world ; and then the idea besieges her that one day she may be taken from that poor crippled creature, which will never be able to fight its battle with the world, and she thinks how much happier it would be if it did not live. In a scene which, for strength, is in our opinion unsurpassed in any play we have seen in recent years, Jean discusses with herself, plans, and executes the deed. She kills her baby, not in an excess of madness, but in the conviction that she does a good action by taking the cripple from the miseries of this life, and

b

uniting it with the man she loved above all men,
her dead husband.   In the third Act the catastrophe
takes place.   Jean pays the penalty of her crime
with her own life.   She pays it cheerfully, not like
a criminal who walks to the scaffold unmoved, but
like a fanatic who dies for her cause.   The parting
between Jean and her mother was so affecting that
old men, as we saw, cried, while women melted in
tears ; and whenever a play produces this effect, it,
we believe, represents a true phase of life.   Artificial
scenes may interest, but they never make one's heart
ache.   *Alan's Wife* is not a cheerful play, but in art
we have no right to ask whether a thing is cheerful
or pleasant, or painful or awe-inspiring : we have
but to ask, Is it art ?   And to deny that *Alan's
Wife*, with its directness, its exquisite writing, its
soul-stirring power, is a work of art, is simply
anathematising tragedy altogether ; for if ever tragedy
has been written by a modern Englishman, *Alan's
Wife* has a right to claim that title.   We know but
one more powerful, modern play, equally sad and
equally simple : Ibsen's *Ghosts*—that is all."

And now that I have read the play once more
in the proof-sheets, I do not retract one word
from what I have said.   *Alan's Wife* is, in my
humble opinion, one of the truest tragedies ever
written by a modern Englishman, and I cannot but
express my regret that I am not able to divulge the
name of the author, which, in deference to my solemn
promise to Miss Robins, I have not even endeavoured
to ascertain.

J. T. GREIN.

Introduction.

BY WILLIAM ARCHER.

Le public n'est pas pessimiste : il ne saurait comprendre la fantaisie
singulière de certains esprits qui voient le monde mauvais, et qui
s'en consolent par le plaisir tout intellectuel et aristocratique de
cette connaissance. . . . Il préfère les plus tragiques horreurs à
certaines cruautés d'observation.—*Jules Lemaître :* "*Les Contem-
porains,*" 2me *Série,* p. 236.

THE author of *Alan's Wife* has deputed to
me the task of relating its history, and,
if need be, of pleading its cause. The
former duty I undertake all the more
readily as I am in great measure responsible for the
existence of the play, and it is only right that I
should put on record my complicity before the fact.
That very complicity, of course, debars me from
appearing in the character of an impartial critic. But
is there such a thing, one may ask in parenthesis, as
impartiality in criticism? Are we not all mere advocates, pleading the cause of our individual prejudices,
predilections, fads, and fancies,—if indeed, we are
fortunate enough to have any personal tastes to
champion, and do not merely hold a brief for some
party, or serve as mechanical mouthpieces for the
prejudices of the compact majority? Be this as it
may, in the present instance I lay no claim to impartiality. It is confessedly as an advocate that I
appear in court. Not simply, or specially, as an

advocate for this play : as will presently appear, I
am in some respects prejudiced *against* the manner
in which the author has treated the subject. It is
for the subject itself—in defence of its right to a place
within the sphere of art—that I address the court.
If the length of my address should appear dispropor-
tionate to its theme, the reader must be good enough
to bear in mind that the case of *Alan's Wife* is in
some sense a test case. A principle—an important
principle—is at stake : the question of the artist's
right to " see life steadily and see it whole." It is
a question, I admit, on which I feel strongly. If,
as some say, it is a disadvantage to an advocate to
approach a case with any ardour of conviction, I
must at once beg the indulgence of the court ; for
I certainly labour under that disability.

It may be well to state clearly, at the outset, that
I am not " instructed " by the author, and do not
pretend to express his personal views, whether
artistic or philosophical. I do not even know what
his views are. Though I, indirectly, suggested the
theme to him, he wrote the play without consulting
me on a single point. It was finished, as it now
stands, before I knew that it was begun. Nor have
I since discussed the matter with him. Some correspondence passed between us as to one or two points
of theatrical expediency, but we have had neither
occasion nor opportunity to go into the deeper
questions involved. His philosophic standpoint is,
in all probability, widely different from mine ; and
in any case, nothing that I say is either inspired or
endorsed by him. In fairness to the author, then, I
would suggest that the reader should, in the mean-

time, skip the rest of this preface, and go straight to the play. After reading it and forming his own estimate of its merits, he may, if so minded, hark back and compare notes with me. These pages are designed to serve as a " reversible " commentary, a prologue and epilogue in one ; and readers who have not seen the play will do best to treat them as an epilogue.

Now for the history of *Alan's Wife*. Some time in April 1891—shortly before the production of *Hedda Gabler*—Miss Elizabeth Robins lent me a Swedish magazine, *Ur Dagens Krönika*, of the previous January, containing a story entitled *Befriad*, by an authoress, hitherto unknown to me, named Elin Ameen. Miss Robins had read the story in a German translation, and had been impressed by it, though not as a subject for theatrical treatment. I too was impressed by it, and kept it by me for some time, with a vague intention of translating it. Then, thinking over it one day, I suddenly " saw " it in the form of a play. It shaped itself naturally, inevitably, into three scenes, of absolute and, as it seemed to me, beautiful simplicity and straightforwardness. A fellow-student of the drama, with whom I had more than once had some friendly controversy with regard to the painful in art, happened to be living near me. To him, by way of experiment, I told the story, asking whether he would like to see it on the stage. As I foresaw, he at once protested in the strongest terms. The thing would be utterly, unspeakably brutal and hideous. Humanity and Jules Lemaître would cry out against it with one voice. That made

the temptation quite irresistible.   There is nothing
in the world I love so much as hearing humanity cry
out in the voice of Jules Lemaître ; so I determined
that the deed should be done.   Accordingly I jotted
down a rough scenario of the play as I saw it, and
sent it to Miss Robins, mentioning the names of two
young dramatists, to one or other of whom I advised
her to suggest the theme.   Then, for a long time, I
heard and thought nothing more of the matter, until
one day Miss Robins informed me that she had acted
on my advice, that one of the dramatists had been
fired by the idea, and that the play was already
written.   She also broke to me, as considerately as
possible, the news that, except as regards the division
into three scenes, my scheme had been entirely thrown
overboard.   On the whole, I could not but admit
that the new form the thing had assumed possessed
many practical advantages.   But I have still a
sneaking tenderness for my original conception ; and
as a comparison between the two will best convey my
technical criticism of the existing play, I will briefly
sketch the play as I saw it.

The scene was to remain in Sweden, and the action
was to be simple and condensed in the highest degree.
In the first scene there were to be only three characters
—the mother, the daughter, and a female neighbour—
not counting, of course, the mute personages passing
on the road, and the little group of workpeople at
the close.   The minister, James Warren, is practically an invention of the English author.   A rejected
suitor of Emma's is mentioned in the original, but
does not appear in person.   The conversation with
Warren, however, is the only serious departure from

my conception in the first scene ; it is in the second scene that the chief difference comes in. After an opening passage between mother and daughter, the district doctor was to have called on his rounds—a burly, benevolent, somewhat coarse-grained man, representing that medical optimism which is not founded upon piety, or indeed upon any metaphysical basis, but springs from a sort of instinctive feeling that the great machine of nature must go on, and that pain and misery are " all in the day's work." The conversation between him and Emma (Jean) was to have been the crucial passage of the play. She was to have questioned him, somewhat minutely, as to the probable future of the child, and in her questions, and her comments on his replies, the audience was to have felt the resolution to end the crippled life growing gradually in her mind, while the burly doctor was to have been placidly convinced that he was pouring balm upon her wounded soul, and leaving her reconciled and comforted. On the doctor's departure, she was to have had a few words —very few almost incoherent words—of soliloquy, and then, in an inner room, seen but vaguely by the audience, she was to have done the deed. As soon as it was over, she was to have rushed out, panic-stricken at the silence of death, called to her mother, and motioned her to go into the inner room ; and then, on the mother's outcry of horror, she was to have said "Yes, I did it," or words to that effect—whereupon, Curtain. The third scene was to have consisted of a mere conversation between Emma and the doctor in her prison cell, several years later. It appears that there is no capital punishment in Sweden,

—in Elin Ameen's story, at any rate, imprisonment for life seems to be regarded as the inevitable consequence of child-murder. Emma was, in the simplest words, to have declared that she desired no commutation of her sentence and had no wish to return to the world from which she felt herself cut off by her terrible act ; but at the same time she was to have declined any expression of remorse or regret for that act, declaring (as Jean actually does), that she had shown the child the only true kindness.

This play would clearly have been more academic, more of a mere experimental exercise, than the one now before us. As regards the first and third scenes, the author has, I gladly admit, improved upon my scheme, humanised and *dramatised* it. My arguments for keeping the scene in Sweden were based, not upon any artistic advantage, but upon mere cowardly expediency. I thought the episode would be less likely to shock people beyond endurance if the scene were removed from their own doors—for impressions of horror are apt to vary inversely as the square of the distance. But the incidents were just as natural in England as anywhere else, and I soon recognised that the author had taken the wiser as well as the bolder part in placing the scene in our own north country. The invention of the "little minister," too, seems to me a happy one. He serves to throw into relief an essential element in Jean's character : her worship of physical strength and beauty, her intolerance of all that is sickly and stunted ; and, at the same time he makes, as it were, an official mouthpiece for the consolatory commonplaces of piety. But I own it is not without a pang

of regret that I compare the existing second scene
with that which I had sketched. The interview
between Emma and the doctor would have been a
subtle piece of intellectual, as opposed to merely
emotional, drama. It would have taken a master
of dialogue to write it, but the thing would have
been worth doing. I think, too, that the end of the
scene as I conceived it would have been at once
more artistic and more effective from the acting
point of view. The transference of the locality to
England made the inner room somewhat improbable,
but that difficulty might have been got over. I had
devised an arrangement of lights during the actual
murder-scene which would, I think, have been im-
pressive; and, altogether, the scene would have been
more finished, less hurried and huddled, than that
which the author has chosen to write. So far as
this whole passage is concerned, in a word, I am
disposed to agree with those critics who find the
drama too much simplified, and hold that thought is
sacrificed to emotion; but, unlike them, I feel that
the fault is redeemed by a very genuine beauty and
poignancy of emotional expression.*

So much for the genesis of the little drama. Let
us now glance at some of the great questions which
it involves. What originally attracted me in the

* The author and I are at variance as to whether in my
scenario (which I have unfortunately destroyed) I had retained
the baptism-scene of the Swedish story. My recollection is
that I had suppressed it, feeling that a woman who was
capable of reasoning as I intended Emma to reason in the
scene with the doctor, would not be likely to concern herself
about infant baptism. The dramatist, on the other hand,
is strongly under the impression that I had retained the

theme, what now attracts me in the play, is precisely
its wealth of ethical and æsthetic suggestion. In
saying this, I do not beg the question of its merits.
It may be artistically feeble and morally repre-
hensible ; it may prove nothing, save that bunglers
rush in where artists fear to tread ; but however crudely, however rashly, however inade-
quately, it does undeniably confront us with some
of the most momentous problems of art and of
conduct.   Ought not criticism to have recognised
this fact, instead of confining itself to almost inarticulate outcries of horror, contempt, and reprobation ?   My present purpose is to do for the critics
what they were too shocked and scandalised to
do for themselves : namely, discover what are the
essential differences between—I will not say this
tragedy, since the term may be held to beg the
question — between this painful play and other
painful plays, ancient and modern, which are, by
common consent, held beautiful and admirable.   I
want (in all sincerity) to understand, and help the critics
to understand, their rejection of the play, and my
acceptance of it.   No one can be argued into liking
a thing he dislikes ; but I am sanguine enough to
hope that some of the critics who most heartily
disliked *Alan's Wife* may be brought to recognise

scene ; and he may be right.   The matter is of no great
moment, one way or the other ; for a great deal of instinctive
superstition may undoubtedly survive even in a very keen
intelligence.   As the play and the characters actually stand,
in any case, the baptism-scene is essential.   Emma Olsen
might or might not have baptised the child ; Jean Creyke
certainly would have.

in it the manifestation of a tendency not altogether contemptible.

Need I apologise for making Mr. A. B. Walkley the spokesman of the opposition? Surely not. If Mr. Walkley objects to having this "bad eminence" thrust upon him, he holds the remedy in his own hands. He has only to write less piquantly, less intelligently, less suggestively—in a word, less like himself—and I, for one, shall never dream of singling him out from the compact majority. While he remains what he is—the most brilliant and entertaining of theatrical theorists—he must submit with a good grace to the drawbacks, if drawbacks they be, of such well-merited distinction. I do not even apologise for applying the rude "teazles" of analysis to the fairy fabric of his impressionism. If, or in so far as, he is an impressionist, it is of set purpose, and not for want of analytic, and even casuistic, faculty. He may now and then affect a sort of butterfly irresponsibility; but there be butterflies that are apter to break the wheel than to be broken on it.

There is no denying that the effect produced upon Mr. Walkley by the performance of *Alan's Wife* was a highly undesirable one. It jarred him out of his natural urbanity, and it impaired his perception of physical fact. This is the exordium of his criticism in the *Star* for Saturday, April 29th :—

When the inevitable and tiresome cry of "author" was raised, at the close of the Independent Theatre Society performance at Terry's last night, Mr. Grein came forward to declare that he did not know the author of *Alan's Wife*—if he did, "he would shake him by the hand." Whereupon a

neighbour of mine in front muttered, " and I would shake him
by the throat." I am by nature of a pacific disposition, but this
time, I am bound to say, I am almost of the same mind as my
neighbour.

It is not without a certain tremor that I even copy
these lines, at this distance of time : what wonder
that when I first read them, hot-and-hot from the
press, my heart was in my boots ? True, I was not
the person directly threatened ; but he, I knew, was
ensconced behind the bastion of anonymity ; and,
failing his throat, I did not know but that the
furibund critic might be tempted to impress his
opinion upon the windpipe of a self-confessed
accessory before the fact. The " almost " somewhat
reassured me ; but for that comfortable adverb,
I should certainly have taken steps to have Mr.
Walkley bound over to keep the peace. And
you, gentle reader, now that the play is before you,
do you feel that such violent measures, or even
violent expressions, are really quite proportionate
to the occasion? *Is* the poor little play such a base
and brutal and utterly abominable thing that, like
Mr. Walkley, you would apply to the author that
terrible line of Dante,

" E cortesia fu lui esser villano ? "

Mr. Walkley, we know, is not easily " villano " to
any one. It must have been a shock indeed that
could thus hustle him out of his habitual courtesy.

And out of his habitual clearness of perception to
boot. After giving an account—a perfectly correct
account—of the end of the first scene, he philoso-
phises as follows :—

Now, here this question I have already hinted at, the question whether art has limitations of subject, at once occurs. If there is no limitation, why is the playwright content with showing us the woman's horror at the thing on the bier? Why not bring the bier down to the footlights and shock us all with it? It would be very easy: a pennyworth of red ochre would do the trick. I leave you to ponder this aspect of the matter, and pass on to Scene 2.

We will consider this argument presently; what I want to note here is that Mr. Walkley "pondered the matter" so profoundly that by the middle of the next week he had convinced himself that the playwright was *not* "content with showing us the woman's horror at the thing on the bier," but did actually "do the trick" with "a pennyworth of red ochre" or other pigment. In *The Speaker* for May 6th, Mr. Walkley roundly asserted that the "case" of *Alan's Wife* was "presented with no attenuation, but rather persistent aggravations of its horrible circumstances. *We are shown the stretcher, the mangled corpse, the child.*" I wrote to the Editor of *The Speaker* (the correspondence is reprinted in the Appendix), pointing out that we were indeed shown the stretcher, but that, as a simple matter of fact, we were not shown the other two blood-curdling objects; whereupon Mr. Walkley retorted, that I, not he, was "strangely mistaken,"—that he saw with his own eyes "the sheet lifted from the man's head and shoulders, which were streaked with paint to indicate some hideous disfigurement." The reader will find in the letters from Miss Robins and Mr. De Lange, reprinted in the Appendix, conclusive proof that, though Mr. Walkley may possibly, by mistake, have been allowed a glimpse of the man who played the corpse, he certainly saw no "hideous disfigurement," because there was none to see. The hallucination is curious in itself; but it becomes doubly so when we find, on comparing his assertions in *The Speaker* of May 6th and May 20th with the above-quoted passage from *The Star* of April 29th, that it was not an optical but a purely mental illusion from which Mr. Walkley suffered. Writing immediately after the production, he asked why the playwright did *not* do what, a few days later, he asserted and reasserted that that gory-minded miscreant actually *did* do. It is perfectly certain that the playwright either was or was not " content with showing us the woman's horror at the thing on the bier." Why did Mr. Walkley begin by asserting the former alternative, and end by staking his veracity on the latter? *Mystère!*

The matter of fact, of course, is no longer in dispute, and Mr. Walkley's good faith never was so for a moment. I advert to the discussion partly because it involves what seems to me a curious psychological phenomenon, throwing a somewhat disquieting light upon the value of evidence; but mainly because it proves beyond a doubt that Mr. Walkley was actually " upset" by *Alan's Wife* to such a degree as to be incapable of discriminating between what he saw and what he imagined. This is, in a sense, a testimony to the skill of the author and of the actress; but it is certainly not the business of art to produce hallucinations. A brief inquiry into the reasons for his frenzy of reprobation may throw some light upon the essential merits or demerits of the play.

Let us note, in the first place, that neither Mr.

Walkley nor any other critic has accused the play
of untruth, unnaturalness, even exaggeration. The
writing is not impugned except on the score of too
great sobriety. According to Mr. Walkley, the
play is

a crude and bald statement of one of those exceptionally
horrible cases which make us wring our hands at the hideous
injustice of life, and cry aloud against the vaunted benevolence
of the Creator as a monstrous imposture. But as such cases
happen, why, you ask, may they not be stated on the stage ?
Well, it is a difficult question. At present I am not prepared
with a reasoned answer. You must give me time. I can only
say now that I feel such things to be outside the province of
art, my instincts revolt against them, they stretch me on the
rack. You think this, possibly, heated, exaggerated language;
but I am quite sincere. I was quite miserable while the
curtain was up last night, and when it was down I had the
relief of waking from some ghastly nightmare. Now, I am for
extending the boundaries of dramatic art, but I object to seeing
it attempting what could be done much more cheaply and
expeditiously by a surfeit of pork chops.

It is only fair to remember that these lines must have
been written in the small hours of the morning, before
the critic had had time to reflect and clarify his
thoughts. If a surfeit of pork chops evokes in
Mr. Walkley's brain " a crude and bald statement of
one of those horrible cases which make us wring our
hands at the injustice of life," then Mr. Walkley is
an even more interesting dreamer than Mr. R. L.
Stevenson, and ought at once to communicate his
" case " to the Psychical Society. The note of the
nightmare is precisely that it is not " crude and bald,"
but that its horror is worked up with all sorts of
fantastic and impossible circumstance. There are
plenty of nightmares in dramatic literature—for

instance, Webster's *Duchess of Malfi* and *White
Devil*, many other Elizabethan plays, by Tourneur,
Marston, and others, and the German and English
ghost-plays which made our grandfathers' flesh creep,
such as Monk Lewis's *Castle Spectre*.   If Mr. Walkley
even chose to denounce the second and third acts of
Gengangere as a nightmare, it would be hard to say
him nay; for there the horror is sedulously elaborated,
and it may even be doubted whether the precise form
of the catastrophe is physically possible.   But in
Alan's Wife the case is stated "crudely and baldly,"
says Mr. Walkley—I prefer to say simply and soberly.
The horrors of the theme are neither physically exhibited (we may take it, I think, that Mr. Walkley
is dislodged from that position), nor insisted on in
words.   The reader may search the text in vain for
a single crudely descriptive expression.   There is
not a word in which the author essays (in Lamb's
phrase) to "touch a horror skilfully," as Ibsen does
in that terrible speech of Oswald's : " It always sets
me thinking of cherry-coloured velvet—something
soft and delicate to stroke."   I think, then, that
Mr. Walkley must allow his pork chops to follow
Alan's mangled remains to that museum of mistakes
which every man, and especially every critic, keeps
somewhere in the background of his memory.   *Alan's
Wife* does not belong to the nightmare category of
plays.   It is excluded from it by the very simplicity
on which the critic insists so strongly—unless, indeed,
Mr. Walkley chooses to class every painful experience
as a nightmare, in which case the illustration loses
all literary value, and becomes a mere piece of bad
style.

Introduction. xxiii

"The piece is in three scenes," Mr. Walkley
continues. "They are not called acts, and they are not
acts, for there is no arrangement or development in
them ; they are raw, not cooked . . . . My criticism
can be condensed into a single syllable—Ugh ! I
declare that there is no art in this thing, no design,
no fusing of the parts in the alembic of the intellect."
This criticism would be a great deal more instructive
if Mr. Walkley had been good enough to indicate
what sort of "cookery" ought to have been applied
to the play. Would he have had the author invent
an intrigue, make the villain (a rejected suitor of
Jean's) set the machinery in motion at the moment
when Alan was under the circular saw, and then
chloroform Jean, smother her baby, and persuade her,
when she regained her senses, that she herself had
done the deed in delirium ? Would this have been
putting the thing through "the alembic of the
intellect" ? Of course not ; Mr. Walkley intends
no such imbecility; but what then *does* he intend ? I
am at a total loss to conceive any further arrangement
of the theme that would not have denaturalised it,
or any "development" that would not have meant
a needless prolongation of the agony. Does Mr.
Walkley complain that he does not know enough of
the characters ? What more does he want to know?
It is true that in the two old women there is no great
depth or subtlety ; but Mr. Walkley has been a
villager himself,—has he observed any great depth or
subtlety in the characters of the cottage matrons, his
neighbours ? They are touched-in with a pleasant
humour which is not, perhaps, so devoid of "art"
as Mr. Walkley imagines. Let him try to draw,

dramatically, two of his aforesaid village neighbours, and he may find it no such child's play. The minister, too, is a very simple character ; but what else should he be? An Arthur Dimmesdale or Robert Elsmere would be utterly out of place in these surroundings. James Warren is an earnest, God-fearing, primitive Christian, drawn without irony or bitterness, and quite fairly representing, to my mind, the pious point of view. Would Mr. Walkley have preferred an abler man, who should state the case for Providence with more emphasis and insistence ? It would have been easy to make the argument wordy and undramatic ; but alas ! I fear Mr. Walkley must agree with me that even the most skilful sophistry would not have mended matters, and would only have prolonged his personal torments. Remains, then, Jean,—do we want more light upon *her* character ? Unless, like Artemus Ward, we are anxious to know whether she has had measles, and if so how many, I fail to see what more we have to learn about her. She is a fresh and sturdy young woman, come of the sound peasant stock which we recognise in her mother, but inheriting a somewhat superior intelligence from her schoolmaster father. She has always been the brightest, cleverest girl of her " set," as we should say, and has thus developed a sort of physical and spiritual pride. Without snobbery, without any desire to " rise in the world," she will not be content with less than the best of what life has to give her. She selects as her mate the handsomest, most capable man of her class that comes in her way ; she makes her home the brightest in the village ; her child is to be the sturdiest, bonniest

bairn in the world. Is not this "character" enough
to satisfy Mr. Walkley? Character, in the artistic
sense, I take to mean natural, probable, justified
differentiation : an individualisation which is neither
fantastic nor arbitrary, but explicable, and, by artistic
methods, explained. Is not Jean, in this sense, a
clearly-drawn character? She is neither a featureless,
conventional puppet, nor an eccentric, bewildering
monstrosity. When calamity falls upon her with a
reduplicated blow, her action is the logical outcome
of the pride and courage—the impatient, intolerant
egoism, if you choose to put it so—which we have
clearly recognised in her beforehand.

> Under the bludgeonings of chance
> Her head is bloody, but unbowed.

You are by no means bound to admire her action,
but, if criticism is in any sense an exercise of the
reason, you are bound to admit or to deny that its
premises are sufficient, and that it is consistent with
its premises. I do not understand Mr. Walkley to
dispute either of these propositions. What, then, does
he mean by the "development" for which he calls
out so loudly?

"Any man who chooses," he goes on, "can take
the bare horrors of life and fling them, pell-mell,
on the stage ; but until we have revised our
dictionaries we cannot call that man a dramatist."
Again I can only appeal to the reader to say whether
the man who has drawn the characters of the two
old women and Jean, who has written the exquisitely
tender scene between Jean and her mother in the

first act (see p. 16), * and has portrayed Jean's despairing rebellion in the second act, can be said to have " flung horrors pell-mell upon the stage." Could "any man who chooses" have conceived the tragic simplicity of Jean's outcry, " Oh, don't tell me about it—don't tell me about any other woman's child ! " or the heartrending pathos of her prayer, ". . . He's so little, dear God, so helpless—and he never did any wrong. *He* hasn't been drunk with life, and strength, and love—he hasn't walked through the world exulting and fearless and forgetting You. That was I, O Father in heaven ! Punish *me*—and take the baby away." Come now, Mr. Walkley, is there absolutely " no art in this thing " ?

The fact is that in all this about " arrangement " and "development" and "art," and " fusing of parts " and "the alembic of the intellect," Mr. Walkley is unwisely issuing from his entrenchments

---

* " *With some lack of delicacy*," says the critic of *The Standard*, writing of this scene, " *she reveals a strictly domestic secret to her mother.*" Let me urge the reader to turn forthwith to the passage in question ; for until he has the text beneath his eyes he cannot admire, as it ought to be admired, the ineffable, the more than seraphic, purity of soul which could prompt such a remark. From what nunnery, I wonder, does *The Standard* recruit its staff? But no ! I will not do the Catholic Church the injustice of supposing that in its most secluded cloister there could be found a mind capable of discovering " some lack of delicacy " in the scene between mother and daughter. Is it not strange and lamentable that the Vivien of Party Spirit should thus be suffered by men (presumably) of intelligence and culture, to raise her voice in a purely literary discussion,

> " Polluting, and imputing her whole self,
>   Defaming and defacing, till she left
>   Not even Lancelot brave, nor Galahad clean."

and exposing himself to fire. He is trying to give reasons for what he admits to be an unreasoning, unreasonable instinct. In suggesting that the theme ought to have been treated otherwise, he implicitly admits that it ought to have been treated at all; whereas the whole strength and validity of his position lies in denying this. The fact is, he does not begin to know how it has been treated. "The drama of infanticide," as he himself puts it, "has knocked all the critical spirit out of him." He fell from the first into a deliquium of nervous horror, which obscured his perception, or at any rate his realisation, of the plainest physical facts; how, then, could he be expected to estimate justly, or even rationally, the artistic merits of the production? In criticising details of workmanship, he was attempting what was unnecessary, and (to one in his state of mind) essentially impossible. He ought simply to have entrenched himself in the syllogism, "What is intolerably painful cannot be artistic; to me *Alan's Wife* is intolerably painful; therefore to me *Alan's Wife* is inartistic." He ought to have said, "I neither know nor care how the play is written —I simply assert that it ought not to have been written at all. My dentist may exhibit consummate skill in drawing my teeth, but I own myself incapable of criticising or appreciating his performance : I take laughing-gas that I may not have to do so. The author of *Alan's Wife* ought, in common humanity, to have administered an anæsthetic."

This position would have been unassailable from the logical side, but still open to criticism from the point of view (1) of fact, (2) of what may be called critical morals. In the first place it is a mere figure of speech to call the pain inflicted by *Alan's Wife* "intolerable." It is not unendurable, because we see that it is endured by a theatre-full of men and women, including Mr. Walkley, and that, except perhaps in temper, nobody is a halfpenny the worse. I have even my own doubts as to whether, if the author had been forthcoming, Mr. Walkley would have taken him by the throat. That, too, has somewhat the air of a figure of speech. The fact is, there is a touch of sophistry, and even of affectation, in the attempt to class these imaginary sufferings with the real pains of life, whether physical or mental. It would certainly conduce to lucidity if we had a separate set of terms for them. And, this being so, may we not question whether the critic has a moral right to let his nerves get the better of his intelligence to such an extent as to make him incapable of accurate assertion and coherent reasoning with regard to any work of art, however humble? Is he not, in some sense, deserting his post when he can find nothing better to say than "Ugh!" (with variations) about such a play as *Alan's Wife*? Mr. Walkley must excuse me if I cannot accept the theory that volition has nothing to do with the matter, and that he simply *cannot* keep his head before even (to accept his own description) "a crude and bald statement" of one of the injustices of life. To a very great degree, we feel what we lay ourselves out to feel. It would have needed but a slight effort on Mr. Walkley's part to have remained "resolute and calm" even at sight of those horrific objects, the stretcher and the cradle.

Was he not bound, for the honour of his craft, to make that effort ? He could then have deprecated the play, if he still felt so disposed, rationally and effectively, doing justice to such merit as it possesses, while arguing, in temperate fashion, that the form of art to which it belongs is, on the whole, undesirable. Is not the critic who refuses calm and courteous consideration to any seriously intended work of art, however mistaken, guilty of infringing the just liberty of artistic experiment ? By all means let us fight for our preferences, according to the rules of the game ; but do not let us claim a suspension of the rules, on the plea of personal disablement, and then shut our eyes and slash around at random.

"But soft !" cries Mr. Walkley, " you are all this time assuming the very point which I deny—namely, that *Alan's Wife* deserves to be classed or treated as a work of art at all." Pardon me : I am not precisely assuming it ; I have tried, as well as I could, to convince the reader that there *is* " art in this thing." But I have not yet quoted the passage in which Mr. Walkley finally excludes the play from the sphere of art. Here it is :—

> Drama, like any other art, deals with ideas ; by ideas it lives and moves and has its being. But there are hateful, intolerable, damnable facts in life which convey no ideas : the mind cannot deal with them, because the force with which they strike us benumbs all thought. They do not interest the spectator ; they stun him. The odious, brutal, cruel malignity of nature, of which *Alan's Wife* gives us an instance, is outside—whether above or beneath I know not—but it is outside the region of art.

One might, perhaps, demand some slight definition of the term " idea " before giving unqualified assent even to the general proposition that art cannot exist apart from ideas. But, admitting that it cannot, what has that to do with *Alan's Wife* ? How is it possible to assert that the play " conveys no ideas " ? By Mr. Walkley's own showing, it conveys at least one very momentous idea—the idea that life, and all that makes life worth living, is for ever at the mercy of brute chance, cruel, capricious, immoral—

> " As flies to wanton boys are we to the gods :
> They kill us for their sport."

Is not that a definite enough idea for Mr. Walkley ? It may be very false—all the theologies and most of the philosophies of the world have been occupied from time immemorial in proving it so — but an idea it certainly is. It is even the idea which underlies almost all tragedy ; for the notion of *tragische Schuld*, the attempt to moralise tragedy, and make suffering correlative with sinning, is a sophistry which I am sure does not deceive so acute a mind as Mr. Walkley's. And not only does the play convey this idea ; it also opens up one of the most solemn and fateful questions of conduct that human life can possibly present. Mr. Walkley himself admits as much, even while appearing to deny it. Read this curious passage from *The Speaker* of May 6th:—

There is no intellectual quality in this play. It presents no ethical thesis, no *crux*, not even any development of character. A poor wretch, maddened by horrible misfortune, her brain still dizzy with the pangs of childbirth, kills her child. Well, this spectacle shocks me, it tears my very heartstrings ; but it gives me nothing to break my mind upon. There is no problem in the case, no outlet for speculation ; it is a hopeless *impasse*. " Not so fast," cries a friend, " you are wrong in calling this woman mad. She is as sane as you or I, and a little more unflinching in her logic. She kills the child deliberately, out of kindness, to save it from the certainty of worse misfortune than death ; and she goes as deliberately to her own death, feeling that she, like her child, is better out of the world. This is not madness, it is reasoned conviction. And as for intellectual problems, what problem could there be more profound than that of the value of human life ? Are there not, admittedly, cases of hopeless mania or incurable disease—cancer, say, or rapid consumption—in which it would be " a mercy " to put sufferers out of their misery at once ? Ask any physician, and he will tell you of many instances in his own experience where the question of " killing—no murder " is at least arguable. This play presents such a case, and so appeals to the intellect. I can only reply that, even if *Alan's Wife* raises this question, it does not thereby stand excused. Such a question is one of the gravest which the human mind can consider ; it is only to be solemnly meditated upon in the privacy of the study. A play is a public act performed under conditions the reverse of solemn. The idea of a number of men and women, in lazy after-dinner mood, sitting at ease in their stalls, extracting a new sensation for their jaded nerves out of such a question as this, treating it as a *chasse* to their coffee or a whet for their supper, is positively nauseous. But, of course, *Alan's Wife* does not raise this question. The most determined advocates for a revision of the popular views on the sacro-sanctity of human life would shrink from arguing that the—possibly beneficent—task of putting a crippled child out of its misery should be confided to the child's own mother. Look at it how you may, I submit that this play ought never to have been written.

Is not this a curious feat of logic? Because Mr. Walkley chooses, in an off-hand sentence, to decide the question, it follows that " of course" the play does not open it up ! Could there be a more delicious contradiction in terms? Imagine a judge who should say, " *Because* I deliver such and such a judgment in this case, *therefore* the case has never been brought

before the court"!   That is exactly Mr. Walkley's
position.   Even supposing his ruling to be beyond
appeal, is it not precisely *Alan's Wife* which has raised
the question and thus secured its final settlement?
But I am afraid there are stiffnecked casuists who
will *not* accept Mr. Walkley's judgment as final, and
will *not* "shrink from arguing" that Jean did right.
Whether such a task "*should be* confided to the
child's own mother" is a further question for consideration: there is not the least doubt that under
existing conditions it is thrust upon her.   If the
child is to be "set free" at all, it is clearly she who
must do it.   She cannot send for the Sanitary
Inspector or move the Court of Chancery for an
order.   Is it not clear, then, that the play does raise
two questions: (1) Did Jean do right under the
circumstances? (2) Ought the circumstances, and
especially the legal circumstances, to be as they are?
Is there nothing here for Mr. Walkley "to break
his mind upon"?   You can always avoid breaking
your mind upon a question by the simple process of
begging it; and that is precisely what Mr. Walkley
has done.

Still more curious, however, is his attempt to show
that if *Alan's Wife* does raise these questions, it
has no business to.   If any one else were to argue
that the "lazy after-dinner mood" of the average
sensual man was to be the ultimate measure of the
intellectual possibilities of drama, I can imagine the
delicate but none the less scornful irony with which
Mr. Walkley would treat him.   If any one else were
to assume that the drama could not, or at any rate
should not in decency, be anything more than a *chasse*

to the world's coffee, Mr. Walkley would be the very man to make him feel sorry he spoke. But I do not rely upon the mere general tendency of Mr. Walkley's writings to prove that, had he been quite himself, he would never have dreamt of thus degrading an art which, with all its drawbacks and limitations, he loves as well as any of us. It so happens that another play raises precisely the question which is raised in *Alan's Wife*, and that of that play, when the majority of the critics were shrieking themselves black in the face in declaring it " outside the region of art," Mr. Walkley was one of the foremost champions. I refer, of course, to Ibsen's *Gengangere*. If it be " positively nauseous " for " a number of men and women, in lazy after-dinner mood " to consider the question whether a mother is justified in taking the life of her hopelessly afflicted son, why did Mr. Walkley omit to be nauseated when *Ghosts* was produced? And why did he not tell us then that " of course *Ghosts* does not raise this question at all," because he (Mr. Walkley) is of opinion that " the task of putting a brain-sick child out of its misery should not be confided to the child's own mother " ? He cannot even reply that when he saw *Ghosts* he was not in a lazy after-dinner, but in an alert before-dinner, mood ; for the first performance of *Ghosts* took place in the evening. One can only conjecture that, for that occasion only, Mr. Walkley, like the Hunters of the Snark, must have breakfasted at afternoon tea and dined on the following day. For the sake of the realistic, and indeed the serious drama of all sorts, it were much to be desired that the critic's mealtimes might be permanently so arranged, and that, in dealing with any form of art higher than Gaiety burlesque, he should be in a position, like Johnson, to subscribe himself "A. B. W., *impransus.*"

One last instance of the disarray into which Mr. Walkley's intelligence is thrown by *Alan's Wife*. In *The Speaker* of July 8th, writing of the production of *Œdipe Roi*, by the Comédie Française, he thus expresses himself :

The playful critic who has rallied me this week for not shrinking in sympathy at the sight of Œdipus and his agony, as I shrank in horror from the brutalities of *Alan's Wife*, is too clear-minded, surely, not to perceive the essential difference between the two cases. The modern play was a piece of crude and ignoble realism : its whole impact was centred in the display of physical suffering. One had the same shock, because one had the same feeling of every-day actuality, in the theatre, as though one had seen a man run over by an omnibus in the Strand outside. But the whole atmosphere of Sophocles' tragedy is too lofty, too remote from modern life, for the spectator ever to be illuded. When Œdipus puts out his eyes I am not in the least pained, because I do not for an instant forget that I am looking at an actor playing a part. The whole thing is as artificial to me as an opera. Moreover, this spectacle of physical suffering is a mere incident in the play, not its be-all and end-all. There is no loss of human dignity ; so that my " pity and terror " have been " purged " in the true Aristotelian sense.

The " playful critic " was I, though I don't know what I have done to merit the epithet ; and I am certainly "clear-minded enough to perceive an essential difference between the two cases," though not that which Mr. Walkley perceives. The difference is— and here again the question is not one of opinion but of fact—that in *Alan's Wife* no " physical suffering " is " displayed " for so much as a single moment, while in *Œdipe Roi* acute and intolerable physical suffering is displayed for something like half an hour, with a lavish employment of that red-ochre which to Mr. Walkley's mind seems to represent " a horror's crown of horror." In *Alan's Wife*, Alan is dead before we even hear of the accident—" After life's fitful fever he sleeps well "—and the baby is supposed to sleep almost as well up to the moment when the curtain falls upon the mother approaching the cradle. Where in all this is that " display of physical suffering " upon which the " whole impact" of the play " was centred "? Who would not gather from Mr. Walkley's words that Alan was brought on shrieking with anguish, that his ghastly mutilations were displayed to the public, that he died in visible torment, perhaps under the surgeon's knife, that the baby was represented as wailing in illness all through the second act, and that finally we assisted at a long and painful smothering-scene on the open stage ? That is how the play would have been arranged had its " impact centred on the display of physical suffering." Sophocles, again, or rather his interpreters in the first theatre in the world, showed us Œdipus with the blood streaming down his face from the empty sockets out of which the eyes had been torn only a moment before. Can you imagine any more ghastly, more appalling, " display of physical suffering "? And observe that it is not at all *necessary* for the purposes of the drama. The *idea* of Œdipus's self-mutilation would be quite sufficiently conveyed if he appeared with a bandage over his eyes, the wounds having been hastily staunched. The truth is that in the Greek tragedy the horror was deliberately heightened by means of the physical display of physical suffering, while the author of the English play, concerned only with the *idea* and not with the physical facts, kept all actual suffering sedulously out of sight. I am not arguing that Sophocles and Mounet Sully were guilty of transgressing the limits of art, and ought to be taken by the throat and " Ugh'd " into penitence. I am only insisting on the stubborn facts of the two cases, as against Mr. Walkley's misrepresentation, not to say inversion, of them. In the interests of the lucidity he so justly prizes, Mr. Walkley ought to remember that it is neither fair nor rational to dwell upon a fantastic *reductio ad absurdum* until it assumes the stability of an actual fact. He began by asking " Why is the playwright content with showing us the woman's horror at the thing on the bier? Why not bring the bier down to the footlights and shock us all with it ?" —and then he proceeded to aver that the playwright had actually done what the critic chose to consider that he might as well have done, and has ever since written of the play on that assumption. Mr. Walkley —though this is almost incredible—may perceive no essential difference between a thing presented to the senses and a thing suggested to the imagination ; but he ought not to write as though his inability to grasp the distinction between an actual and a supposititious fact were sufficient of itself to make the supposititious fact actual.

If Mr. Walkley really requires to be told why the playwright " was content " to show the bier without showing the mangled body, I will try to satisfy his curiosity. There were clearly three courses open : (1) What would have been called in Greek tragedy a "messenger scene," a "récit de Théramène," a verbal account of the accident. (2) The bringing on of the body, so that Jean should see it, but the audience should not. (3) The open display of the mangled corpse both to Jean and to the audience. These are totally distinct alternatives, and it is folly to pretend that 2 and 3 are practically identical, any more than 1 and 2, or 1 and 3. But what was the object to be gained? What was the function of the scene in the economy of the play? Surely to show Jean's terrible "peripeteia" from exultant happiness to abject misery, and at the same time to make us realise the shock to her system which resulted in the second "bludgeoning of chance," the deformity of her child. Now how was this end to be compassed at once effectually and (to the audience) humanely, or, in other words, in the most artistic fashion? Method 3 was at once out of the question; there was no reason in the world why the audience should see the mangled corpse. Method 1 would either have been totally ineffective and unconvincing, or else far more painful than the method actually chosen. Mr. Walkley himself would scarcely have been satisfied if some one had simply come in and announced "Your husband has been killed at the works," and the curtain had fallen on that unvarnished statement; and, on the other hand, a lengthened breaking of the news and description of the accident would have been agonising if well done, tedious if ill done, and in either case very imperfectly premonitory of Jean's second disaster. I submit, then, that in selecting Method 2, in subjecting Jean and the audience to a "short, sharp shock,"

the author chose precisely the right, the artistic,
compromise between feebleness and brutality.

All this argument, however, leaves untouched
the one essential fact that *Alan's Wife* aroused
nothing but violent antipathy in a very able and
usually very candid critic, who has again and again
shown keen discrimination, delicate sympathy, and
unimpeachable openness of mind, in dealing with
plays of far greater intellectual calibre than this.
I have tried to show that the reasons he himself
alleges for this antipathy are untenable, inconsistent,
and founded, in great measure, on misapprehensions
of fact. But the antipathy remains undeniable,
though Mr. Walkley may have failed to provide an
adequate explanation of it. That very failure is a
testimony to its uncontrollable vehemence. We
have clearly not got at the root of the matter until
we have discovered the real reasons why *Alan's Wife*
has managed to throw such a critic into such a
state of mind. In these real reasons, if we can
only find them, must lie the vindication or con-
demnation of the play. Let us set about the search.
There are two clearly recognised and accepted
(though not always clearly distinguishable) orders
of tragedy : the tragedy of Fate, and the tragedy of
Free-Will, or in other words of Character. Antique
tragedy, broadly speaking, belongs to the former
order, modern tragedy to the latter. Now, in both
of these forms of tragedy, our instinct provides us
with a palliative or palliatives for the pain they
inflict upon us. Out of these presentations of the
evil of life, the alchymy of our "will to live"

extracts, by irrational and illusory but none the less effectual methods, a certain sense of comfort and reassurance. The feelings which induce us not only to endure but to delight in pictures of the night side of life are so complex that it would need a volume rather than a paragraph to unravel them ; but some of the main threads of the tangle may be picked out with comparative ease.

Antique tragedy had of course a religious and and patriotic attraction for its original audiences ; and even in its purely-human aspect, its terrors were mitigated by the remoteness and dignity of its themes. Even to the Athenians, the mythic past of their race seemed indefinitely far off. "There were giants in those days," thought the burgess of Athens, as he saw the cothurnate figures of demigods, heroes and kings stalking across the empurpled scene. He contrasted his own gay, commonplace, civilised life with the fate-haunted existences of these "mighty monarchs in their misery dead," and he felt a new sense of security in the humbleness of his lot. Great crimes, awful retributions, tragic destinies as a whole, seemed the exclusive appanage of a long-extinct generation of superhuman beings.* And

* This is in apparent conflict, I am aware, with Aristotle's theory of pity and terror as expounded by Lessing; but if Lessing's exposition be as just as it is ingenious, it is evident that Aristotle must have been speculating on the effect of ideal tragedy upon an ideal hearer rather than examining into the psychology of an actual audience. Moreover, it might not be impossible, though it would certainly be tedious, to reconcile the Lessing-Aristotle theory with that above stated. It is all a matter, no doubt, of the different planes of consciousness or sub-consciousness.

d

this feeling is naturally even stronger in us moderns
than in the ancients.   The tragedy of Fate is, to us,
entirely unreal.   As Mr. Walkley very truly says
of the *Œdipus Tyrannus*, "its whole atmosphere is
too lofty, too remote from modern life, for the
spectator ever to be illuded."   We are willing to
conceive that at Thebes or Mycenae, at Dunsinane
or even at Ravenswood, men may have been the
playthings of a blind fore-ordinance, essentially
immoral, though sometimes masking its caprices
under a hypocritical show of retributive justice ; but
we instinctively relegate the operation of such a
power to bygone, and generally to mythic, ages,
and conceive it as affecting only a very limited class
of persons of exalted and even semi-divine lineage.
With modern and middle-class mankind, Destiny has
nothing to do.   It would be the very extravagance
of burlesque to represent the House of Smith, like
the House of Pelops, blindly working out the
decrees of Fate.   We trace these legends back to
their source in primitive folk-lore, and regard them
as mere glorified nursery-tales.   Their bearing upon
actual life is symbolic, not direct and practical.
They have literally " no terrors for us."

To this class of tragedies *Alan's Wife* clearly does
not belong.   It does not deal with a mythic past
or with a race of demigods.   It does not postulate
a malevolent personal Power, as fabulous as the
chimæra to our reason, and even to our superstition
as extinct as the megalosaurus.   All the alchymy of
our inborn optimism can extract from it no illusion
of security, no gleam of reassurance.   It inverts the
Horatian warning, and reminds us that not Fate,

but Fatality, visits the cabins of the poor no less than the towers of kings. It allows us none of the Lucretian "suavity" of watching from the shore the struggles of doomed seafarers in the jaws of the deep. We feel that we are all in the same boat, and that is the very feeling which some of us, most of us, resent, and would like to strangle. Then, when it eludes our clutches, we propose, as the next best form of protest, to throttle the wretch who inflicted it upon us.

Where, now, lies the solace, the palliative in modern tragedy, the tragedy of Free-will or of Character? Why, simply in the feeling which the poet has thus artlessly expressed : "Be warned in time by others' harms, and you shall do full well." There is always a moral to the tragedy of free-will, and poor humanity has a touching faith in morals. *Othello* waves like a red flag over the pitfall of jealousy, *Lear* flashes like a lurid danger-signal on the down gradient of doting confidence and senile thirst for lip-homage. In most cases, too, we can relieve our overwrought feelings by execrating the villain or villains—Iago, Claudius, Edmund, Goneril, Regan, Iachimo. No one who has frequented our melodramatic theatres—and melodrama is only bastard tragedy—can doubt the reality and acuteness of this childish satisfaction. Here is a visible, tangible object on which to wreak our vengeance for the discomfort inflicted on our sensibilities. We are even spared the personal trouble of taking him by the throat. We sit quietly by and see him hoist with his own petard—stabbed, poisoned or handcuffed as the case may be—and we go on our

way with the comfortable assurance that "though
the mills of God grind slowly, yet they grind
exceeding small." Even where, as in *The Second
Mrs. Tanqueray*, there is no out-and-out villain, and
the moral is an indefinite one, we feel that we have
been shown faults of character to be avoided, and have
received a lesson which is none the less useful and
important because it eludes formulation in a single
phrase. The tragedy of character, in short, appeals
to our utilitarian instincts. It makes for righteous-
ness or for worldly wisdom. It gives us a sense of
reassurance which is not always or altogether illusory.
If our heart-strings have been wrung, they have not
been wrung in vain.

But *Alan's Wife* is not a tragedy of character.
Jean does not suffer either because she is virtuous or
because she is vicious. There is no warning for us
in her calamity, for nothing she could have done
or left undone would have averted it. There is no
villain for us to take by the throat, for we cannot
wreak vengeance upon intangible, impersonal Fatality.
It has us in its clutches, not we it; and, very
naturally, we do not relish the predicament.

This, then, is the upshot of the matter : *Alan's
Wife* belongs to a third tragic category, not yet
recognised by official criticism—we may call it the
tragedy of Fatality. It is quite open to Mr. Walkley
to say, " I decline to accept tragedy without its
consolations and palliations, real or illusory. I
protest against having my heart-strings wrung to no
practical end. Your tragedy of Fatality depresses and
irritates me. I will have none of it ! Take it away !"
If he had thus decreed *la mort sans phrase*, without

venturing upon a further, and, as I have tried to show, a mistaken analysis of his sensations, his logical position would, as aforesaid, have been inexpugnable, and he would certainly have had the vast majority on his side. But I am, as he was in his time, an advocate of "minority representation" in art. I claim the right of the minority to look at and reproduce life in its own fashion. By all means let the majority lodge its protest; but why should it take the form of inarticulate noises, misrepresentations of fact, and threats of personal violence?

Is it, after all, so utterly inconceivable to a mind like Mr. Walkley's, that there should be a *plaisir tout intellectuel et aristocratique* in the mere constatation and realisation, from time to time, of the clumsy and blundering cruelties of life? He may perhaps suspect me of affecting this feeling because I believe it to be "intellectual and aristocratic"; but the suspicion is quite unjust. The pleasure is to me as natural and unfactitious as a child's delight in sugar-candy. It is true that there is no consolation, no encouragement in *Alan's Wife*, save only the supreme consolation that "The rest is silence." I should be sorry even to assert that the study of fatality in art will help us to bear it rationally and manfully should it come upon us in real life. It is not impossible; but I do not pin my faith to any such utilitarian plea. I appeal direct to the absolute experience of a small, but not numerically negligable or intellectually despicable, minority. Do we not find a peculiar and instinctive satisfaction in now and again facing fairly and squarely the very grimmest facts of life? Have we not a certain sense—an illusion, if you will—of added human dignity when, renouncing the "consolations" of stereotyped sophistry, we have recognised and made up our minds to the immitigable cruelty of "the bludgeonings of chance"? In witnessing such a play as *Alan's Wife*, do we not seem to be looking life straight in the eyes and saying, "There, you great bully! We know you! We are not taken in by your cajoleries! Now go ahead and do your worst!" That this is a rational or admirable attitude of mind, I am far from asserting; it may even be called a sort of cheap posturing, as of Ajax defying a stage thunderbolt; but I own to taking a certain foolish pleasure in it. And, however childish this attitude of mine may be, it behoves even the wisest of us to adopt *some* attitude towards the sheer horrors of life. Philosophy cannot simply ignore them; and art, to my thinking, is conterminous with philosophy—in other words, nothing human is alien to it. Why, then, should we despise and reject a play which brings us face to face with one of the darkest problems of existence —the problem of undeserved, fortuitous, purposeless suffering—and treats it delicately, tenderly, humanely, without any of that savage and cynical pessimism which pervades the works of the Théâtre-Libre playwrights? It will of course be represented that because I praise *Alan's Wife* I want to see the drama entirely given over to gloom and horror. That is mere nonsense. Such works should be exceptional in art, as such miseries are exceptional in life. Only I decline to exclude from the province of art any work which speaks from heart and brain to heart and brain, in however agonising accents.

Before bringing this long discussion to a close, I must qualify my admission that *Alan's Wife* is not a tragedy of character. Jean, in the second act, becomes a moral, or immoral, agent ; her conduct compels us to reflect upon one of the most moment-ous of ethical problems ; our heart-strings have *not* been wrung to no purpose. It is the very awfulness of the problem that leads many critics, and Mr. Walkley among the number, to ignore or elude it. Mr. Walkley, as we have seen above, simply begs the question and goes on his way rejoicing; other critics assume that a mother who can possibly kill her child must be out of her mind, and talk about " puerperal mania," studies in insanity, and so forth. Of course this is partly their fun ; but some of them appear seriously to believe that we are intended to regard Jean Creyke as insane. Nothing, I am sure, could be further from the intention of either Swedish authoress or English author. Every stage in the process of thought and feeling that leads Jean up to her terrible deed is as clear daylight. This facile verdict of insanity is worthy only of a coroner's jury, not of a critical College of Justice. Immediately a cry of horror is raised : " What ! she is not insane ! Then we are asked to applaud her action, and to admit that all deformed children ought to be smothered !" Surely not. Since when have we been expected to approve every sane action that is presented on the stage ? There is a vast space of intermediate ground between a criminal lunatic and an ideal heroine held up for imitation ; and to cover that space at one leap is surely to beat the record in ratio-cinative athletics. Jean Creyke, certainly, is neither

lunatic nor heroine.   She is a terribly afflicted woman,
that is all, who acts as, somewhere or other in the
world, some similarly tortured creature is doubtless
acting at the very moment when I write these words.
Doubtless, too, there are thousands of other women
bearing even greater burdens with stupid resignation
or with cheerful fortitude.   All three phases—the
rebellious, the callous, and the stoical—are in themselves equally interesting, but the rebellious phase
happens to be by far the most dramatic.   It is not
in the least necessary that we should either approve
or condemn Jean's action.   To my thinking the great
tragic value of the theme lies in the fact that we
can do neither with a whole heart.   If you want to
know my own private sentiment on the subject
(though that is quite beside the artistic question), I
think with Jean that she must die, that life is impossible to her after such an act, but that hers is a
case for the lethal chamber which Mr. George R. Sims
was commending the other day rather than for the
common gallows.   But there is not the slightest
reason why one's own particular judgment of the case
of conscience should affect one's estimate of the work
of art.   Our appreciation of the *Choëphori* does not
depend (does it ?) upon our approval or disapproval
of Orestes' matricide.   Some may applaud it, some
condemn ; the majority, probably, feel with me that
the   situation   stands   on   the   highest   tragic   plane
precisely because we can neither freely applaud nor
condemn utterly ; but all three parties are at one in
recognising the greatness of the tragedy.   Well,
Alan's Wife is a little tragedy, not a great one ;
but Jean Creyke has this in common with Orestes,

that she is placed in one of those agonising dilemmas where it seems equally impossible, equally inhuman, to act or to refrain. If she were insane, the ethical problem would vanish, and we should have nothing but a study in mental pathology. I don't say that that might not have its interest, but it is not the interest at which the author has aimed.

Another friend of mine, whose opinion of the play is but little higher than Mr. Walkley's, takes very different ground against it. So far from thinking the theme too horrible for artistic treatment, he objects that far too much fuss is made about it. He writes as follows :

I believe the real difference between us is caused by the play being real to me in a way that it is not to you, or to the author. To you the incident is imaginary ; now to me it is comparatively common. Women do, as a matter of fact, polish off invalids and children on the ground that it is the most sensible and humane thing to do. Infanticide on that and other grounds is not a thing that women confess to ; but every coroner knows how frequent it is. And the women are not at all uncommon who, if they don't exactly give Oswald the morphia, nevertheless deliberately and affectionately read the doctor's instructions backwards. Such women are not in the least like Jean, and never do it in Jean's way. They don't get hung ; and they don't repent: on the contrary, they are invariably proud of having done the right thing. The tragedy, if there is a tragedy, lies in the thing itself, and not in the fuss that is made about it. To represent a woman killing her child in such a way as to convince nine-tenths of the audience that she is suffering from puerperal mania, and then getting hung for it, is to my mind shirking the problem as completely as it can be shirked without ignoring it altogether.

If I were to treat the subject, I should represent Jean as a

rational being in society as it exists at present; and I should
show her killing the child with cool and successful precautions
against being found out. I should then represent her mother
and the parson and all the neighbours as being morally certain
that she had done it, and herself as keeping up no greater
pretence to the contrary than might be needed to save her neck.
And I should represent their theories as to their own horror
and her remorse as breaking down signally in practice, leaving
her, when she had recovered from the natural grief produced
by the sawing episode and so forth, the happiest and most
sincerely respected woman in the parish.

I wish Mr. —— would write his play, or rather
his novel, for I defy him to construct a possible play
on the lines he indicates; but I cannot see why,
because one author would treat a theme in one
way, another author must not treat it in another.
Mr. ——, like Mr. Walkley, though in the opposite
sense, is simply begging the question. " Jean clearly
ought not to have killed the child," says the one
critic, " therefore the question has not been raised."
" She ought to have killed the child in cold blood,
and ought not to have been hung for it," cries the
other critic, "therefore the question is completely
shirked." What is this but the good old British
habit of treating a drama as though it were a political
oration, and applauding or hissing it, without any
thought of its dramatic value, according as one
happens to agree or disagree with its practical con-
clusions? It may be quite true that some women
are capable of performing a compassionate murder
with calm deliberation, and, like the princess in the
fairy tale, living happily ever afterwards; but it is
at least equally certain that many women have not
attained that pitch of philosophy. Why blame the

author of *Alan's Wife* for having chosen to depict
one of the latter class ? Jean Creyke's case is of
everyday occurrence, only that, as a rule, the mother
takes or tries to take her own life as well. It happens
that purely intellectual action interests Mr. ——
more than emotional action ; but that is surely no
adequate reason for demanding that art shall confine
its attention to "strong-minded women," and decline
to take any account of the weaklings who shrink
in anguish from killing a kitten, much more from
killing a child. Observe, too, that the women who,
according to Mr. ——, are "not in the least like
Jean," are not so very unlike her after all. " They
don't repent," he says ; "on the contrary they are
invariably proud of having done the right thing."
This "invariably" is delicious, and throws a flood
of light upon the critic's method of conceiving human
nature. But we need not go into that at present,
for, as it happens, Jean faithfully follows the "in-
variable" rule. She does *not* repent ; she *is* proud
of having done the right thing ; she says so as
emphatically as any human being can. Therefore
Mr. ——'s only real quarrel with her is that she
consents to be hung, instead of living happily ever
afterwards. No doubt that is weak of her ; but we
read in every newspaper of people who elaborately,
and at great personal inconvenience, take their own
lives for comparatively trifling reasons : why should
Mr. —— feel outraged because Jean, after her
double calamity, welcomes the legal means of exit
from a scene on which her part has been so painful ?
The fact that she is .willing to die has nothing to
do with the question whether the law does right to

kill her. That is one of the questions which the
play calls upon us to consider, and Mr. —— has
every right to express his opinion on the point.
But an author cannot justly be accused of "shirking"
a problem because he does not argue it out in all
its aspects and lay down a definite theory on every
point that arises. A play, after all, is a play, not
a discussion-forum. It is the author's business, by
means of a picture of life, to set us thinking,
not to do all our thinking for us. This is what
Mr. —— is too apt to forget.

And now, as I look at the pile of manuscript
before me, I feel that some apology is due to the
reader, for the glaring disproportion between the
prologue and the play. To tell the whole truth, it
is the shortness of the play that is chiefly to blame
for the length of this introduction. I knew that the
publishers were desirous of making the book more
or less uniform in point of bulk with the first volume
of the series—Mr. Shaw's *Widowers' Houses*—and
consequently let my pen run on, at its own discretion
or indiscretion, in the unwonted enjoyment of indefinite space. At the same time, I have not, like
Dogberry, bestowed " *all* my tediousness " upon the
reader. The foregoing brief discussion of the two,
or three, orders of tragedy embodies the essence of
some fifty folios of manuscript which I cut out as
soon as I realised that they did not contain one single
mention of *Alan's Wife,* and formed, in fact, a
separate essay on " The Paradox of Tragedy." For
this heroic excision I claim the reader's gratitude ;
but I am myself none the less grateful to the authors

—Swedish and English—of *Alan's Wife*, for having stimulated me to think out the paradox in question. Like Mr. Walkley, I am all for lucidity; there is no greater delight in life, it seems to me, than (adapting a line of Davenant's) "to follow truth through labyrinths of the mind." And is not this Paradox of Tragedy one of the very strangest in life? But that habit has blunted the wonder of the thing, who would not hold it incredible that mankind—poor purblind humanity, stumbling, along a path beset with pitfalls, from the night to the night—should choose, in its brief rests by the way, to recreate itself with gazing into imaginary abysses? Strange it is indeed—strange and pathetic. The galley-slave may be doomed, in his dreams, to tug a still heavier oar than that to which his body is chained; but why do we wilfully and deliberately (or so it seems) conjure up again and again those dreams of ours which we call *Agamemnon*, and *Antigone*, and *Othello*, and *Lear*, and *Phèdre*, and *Tristan und Isolde*, and *Gengangere*? If you think of it for a moment, is it not much more astonishing that any of us should find *King Lear* endurable than that some of us should find *Alan's Wife* unendurable? No candid reader, I hope, will accuse me of any such absurdity as ranking this poor little play among the tragic masterpieces of literature. Its "total cerebration," in the jargon of the day, is trivial beside that which goes to a serious play by Dumas or Pinero, to say nothing of Wagner or Shakespeare. Moreover, what credit we can allow to the actual brain-work of the play, has to be divided between the Swedish novelist and the English playwright. But a very small voice, with courage, insight, and sincerity behind it, may ask a very great question. *Alan's Wife*, to my thinking, asks two great questions, one ethical the other æsthetic. That is why I am so vehement, and perhaps I should add so prolix, in its defence.

TERRY'S THEATRE,

STRAND, W.C.

THE INDEPENDENT THEATRE.

FOUNDER AND SOLE DIRECTOR, J. T. GREIN.

SECOND SEASON, TENTH PERFORMANCE.

TUESDAY, 2nd *May*, 1893,

ALAN'S WIFE,

A STUDY IN THREE SCENES, FOUNDED ON A STORY BY

ELIN AMEEN.

DRAMATIS PERSONÆ.

Jean Creyke	MISS ELIZABETH ROBINS.
Mrs. Holroyd (Jean's Mother)	MRS. E. H. BROOKE.
Mrs. Ridley	MRS. EDMUND PHELPS.
1st *Woman*	MISS MABEL HARDY.
2nd *Woman*	MISS ANNIE SAKER.
Jamie Warren . . .	MR. JAMES WELCH.
Colonel Stewart . . .	MR. MERVYN HERAPATH.
Roberts (Chief Warder) . .	MR. WALLER.
1st *Warder*	MR. CHARLES GREEVEN.
2nd *Warder* . . .	MR. E. G. WALLER.

The Play produced under the direction of
MR. H. DE LANGE.

The Action of the Play takes place in a Village in the North of England, at the PRESENT DAY.

Alan's Wife.

SCENE I.

A village street runs transversely from front corner, R, *to back,* L. *At right angles to it, starting from front corner,* L, *the outside of a workman's cottage. Door leading to passage: a window on each side of it, through which glimpses can be obtained of cottage interior. The central portion of the stage, in the angle between the street and the cottage, represents the cottage garden, shut off from the street by a low fence with a gate in it. A bench runs along the cottage wall: by it a table, on which are piled up plates, knives, etc., ready for the table to be laid.*

> (*Mrs. Holroyd discovered sitting on bench outside house to the right of door, knitting. People passing along the street. Two men pass with a little child between them, then a little girl, then a woman carrying a child.*)

Woman.

(*as she passes to Mrs. Holroyd*)   A fine day!

I

Mrs. Holroyd.

(*nodding*)   Ay, it's a fine day !   (*The woman passes on.*)

Mrs. Ridley.

(*comes along with a basket on her arm—she stops*)
Good morning, Mrs. Holroyd !

Mrs. Holroyd.

Good morning to you, Mrs. Ridley : it's a warm day !

Mrs. Ridley.

And you look very comfortable there.

Mrs. Holroyd.

Yes, it's nice out here—sit you down and rest a bit ; you'll be tired after your marketing.

Mrs. Ridley.

(*sitting down by her on the seat*)   Well, I don't say I won't be glad of a rest.   It's fine to see you settled in your daughter's house for a bit, like this.

Mrs. Holroyd.

It's the only place I do feel settled in, now she's married.   I just feel lost in my own house without her.

Mrs. Ridley.

Ay, you will that.   It's bad when lassies take up with their husbands and leave their mothers alone.

Mrs. Holroyd.

Ay, you may well say so !   And Jean is all I have. I never had a lad of my own, or another lass either, and it's hard to be left when one is getting into years.

Mrs. Ridley.

Still, you must be glad she has got a good husband, that can work hard and give her all she wants.

Mrs. Holroyd.

Ay, Alan Creyke's a fine fellow, no doubt, and they say he'll soon be foreman. But I did think my Jean would have looked higher. I always thought she would marry a schoolmaster, as I did, or even a minister,—seeing all the book-learning she got from her poor father. She knows as much as any lady, I do believe.

Mrs. Ridley.

Ay, it's wonderful what the books 'll do. They say young Mr. Warren, that's just come to the chapel here, has got more book-learning than the schoolmaster himself, and can talk about it so as no one can understand him. Eh, but it's fine to know as much as that !

Mrs. Holroyd.

(*with a sigh*) It is indeed ! And, Mrs. Ridley, as sure as you see me sitting here beside you, there was a time when that young man was after our Jean, and she might have been the mistress of yon pretty house near the chapel, instead of living in a cottage like ·this.

Mrs. Ridley.

Dear, dear ! To think of that ! Ah well, it's no wonder you're put about at the way she chose.

Mrs. Holroyd.

I don't say that Alan isn't a good husband, mind you, and a good worker too—only I did hope to see my girl a bit grander than she is, as mothers will.

Mrs. Ridley.

Ah well, young people will do their own way.
You must just make up your mind to it, Mrs. Holroyd. I fear the book-learning doesn't go for much
with the lassies, where a fine fellow like Creyke is
concerned—and after all, as to the cottage, it's a nice
little place, and she keeps it beautiful!

Mrs. Holroyd.

She does that—and she wouldn't be her mother's
daughter if she didn't. And the pleasure she takes
in it, too! keeping it as bright and shining as if
there were five or six pair of hands to do it! She
and Allan are nobbut two children about it, and their
house is just like a new toy.

Mrs. Ridley.

Well, that's right! let them be happy now, poor
things; they'll leave it off soon enough.

Mrs. Holroyd.

Eh, yes, I doubt they will, like other folk.

Mrs. Ridley.

Where is Jean? I should like to wish her good
morning. Is she in?

Mrs. Holroyd.

Yes, she's in the kitchen, I believe. (*Calls*) Jean,
Jean! What are you doing, honey? Here's a
neighbour come to see you.

Jean.

(*from within room to the* L) I'll come directly. I'm
getting Alan's dinner ready. I can't leave the sauce-
pan.

Mrs. Ridley.

(*smiling*) Ay, getting Alan's dinner ready! That's the way of it.

Mrs. Holroyd.

Yes, it's always Alan's dinner, or Alan's tea, or Alan's supper, or Alan's pipe. There isn't another man in the North gets waited on as he does.

Mrs. Ridley.

Eh, but that's what he'll want to keep him in his home; they're bad to please, is the men, unless you spoil them. (*Bell begins to ring outside.*) There's the mid-day bell from the works. Creyke 'll soon be here now—I must be getting home too.

Mrs. Holroyd.

Eh, now, but Jean would have liked to shake hands with ye. (*Calls*) Jean! Jean! Be quick, child!

Jean.

(*from within*) Just ready, mother—I'm lifting it off the fire.

Mrs. Ridley.

(*looking along the street*) And in the nick of time too, for here are the men. (*Two or three men walk past.*) Yes, hurry up, Jean, or your man will be here before his dinner's ready.

Jean.

(*from within*) No, no, he won't. (*Appears in door-way of cottage.*) Here it is! (*Comes out carrying a large smoking dish in her hand, which she puts on the table.*) There! How are you, Mrs. Ridley? (*Shakes hands with her.*)

Mrs. Ridley.

Nicely, thank you. And are you going to get your dinner outside then?

Jean.

Yes, indeed; let's be in the air while we can— it's not often we have it as fine as this.

Mrs. Holroyd.

I never saw such a lass for fresh air! and Alan is just as bad.

Mrs. Ridley.

Well, they'll take no harm with it, I daresay; fresh air is bad for nowt but cobwebs, as the saying is.

Jean.

(*laughs*) Ah, that's true enough! (*arranging table*) Now then, if that isn't a dinner fit for a king!

Mrs. Ridley.

And I'll be bound, if it is, you won't be thinking it too good for your husband.

Jean.

Too good! I should think not! Is anything too good for him? Is anything good enough?

Mrs. Holroyd.

(*smiling*) Ah, Jean, Jean!

Jean.

Well, mother, you know quite well it's true! Isn't he the best husband a girl ever had? And the handsomest, and the strongest?

Mrs. Holroyd.

Ah, yes, he's all that, I daresay.

Jean.

(*vigorously wiping tumblers*) Well, what more do you want?

Mrs. Holroyd.

Ah, my dear, as I've often told you, I should like you to have looked higher.

Jean.

Looked higher! How could I have looked higher than Alan?

Mrs. Holroyd.

I wanted to see you marry a scholar.

Jean.

We can't all marry scholars, mother dear—some of us prefer marrying men instead. (*Goes into house.*)

Mrs. Ridley.

The lass is right—there must be some of that sort that there may be some of all sorts, as the saying is; and, neighbour, you must just make the best of it, and be pleased with the man that's made her look so happy. (*Getting up.*)

Mrs. Holroyd.

(*smiling*) Ay, she looks bright enough, in all conscience. (*Jean comes back with cheese and butter on a dish.*)

Mrs. Ridley.

(*smiling at Jean*) She does that, indeed! Well, you won't have to wait long for him now, honey. Here they come down the road, and I must get back to my two lads. Good day to you both. (*Exit through garden gate and up street, to the* L, *exchanging greetings with passing workmen.*)

Jean.

(*cutting bread*) Scholar, indeed ! Mother, how can you say such things before folks ? I know what you mean when you say scholar—yon minister, poor little Jamie Warren.

Mrs. Holroyd.

Ah, Jean, how can you speak so ! He's a man who is looked up to by everybody. Didn't he go up to the big house last Christmastide, to dinner with the gentry, just like one of themselves ?

Jean.

Well, that's right enough if it pleased him, but I shouldn't care to go among folk who thought themselves my betters. (*look from Mrs. Holroyd*) No, I shouldn't. I like Jamie, and have done ever since we were boy and girl together ; but it's a far cry to think of taking him for my master ! no, mother, that's not my kind. (*Goes to tub under the window, wrings out tea cloths and hangs them on picket fence.*)

Mrs. Holroyd.

Ah, Jean, what would your poor father have said ! When you and Jamie used to play together on the village green and go to school together, and Jamie was minding his books and getting all the prizes, your father used to say, " When that lad grows up, he'll be the husband for Jean—he's a good lad, he never gets into mischief; he's never without a book in his hand."

Jean.

Ah, poor father ! but what would *I* have done with a good boy who never got into mischief !

(*laughs*) No, I always knew it wasn't to be Jamie. Why, I remember as far back as when Jamie and I used to come from school, and I'd rush on before and go flying up on the moors, to find the stagshorn moss, with the heathery wind in my face, and hear the whirring summer sounds around us, I used to want to shout aloud, just for the pleasure of being alive—and Jamie, poor little creature, used to come toiling up after me, and call out, "Not so fast, Jean, I'm out of breath, wait for me!" And *I* used to have to help *him* up!

Mrs. Holroyd.
Well, perhaps he couldn't run and jump as well as you, but he had read all about the flowers and plants in his book, and could tell you the names of every one of them.

Jean.
Ay, their names, perhaps; but he couldn't swing himself up to the steep places where they grew to pull them for me. He was afraid—afraid! while I, a girl, didn't know what it was like to be afraid. I don't know now.

Mrs. Holroyd.
Maybe—but he would have been a good husband for all that!

Jean.
Not for me. I want a husband who is brave and strong, a man who is my master as well as other folks'; who loves the hills and the heather, and loves to feel the strong wind blowing in his face and the blood rushing through his veins! Ah! to be happy—to be alive!

Mrs. Holroyd.

Oh, Jean, you always were a strange girl! (*Two men pass.*)

Jean.

Ah, mother, can't you see how fine it is to have life, and health, and strength! Jamie Warren, indeed! Think of the way he comes along, poor fellow, as though he were scared of coming into bits if he moved faster! And the way Alan comes striding and swinging down the street, with his head up, looking as if the world belonged to him! Ah! it's good to be as happy as I am!

Mrs. Holroyd.

Well, you silly fondy! In the meantime, I wonder what Alan is doing this morning? Yon fine dinner of his will be getting cold.

Jean.

Indeed it will. I wonder where he is! (*Men pass.*) All the men seem to have passed. (*Stands just outside the door and looks down the street to the* R, *sheltering her eyes from the sun. Hutton, a workman, passes, and stops to speak to her.*)

Hutton.

Good morning, Mrs. Creyke : a fine day again!

Jean.

It is indeed, Mr. Hutton. What's got my husband this morning, do you know? Why is he so long after the rest?

Hutton.

He's stayed behind to see about something that's gone wrong with the machinery. It's the new saw,

I believe—that's what happens when folks try to improve on the old ways. I don't believe in improvements myself, and in trying these new-fangled things no one can understand.

Jean.

No one? I'll be bound Alan understands them well enough.

Hutton.

Well, happen he does, more than most, and that's why the manager called him back to fettle it up—but I doubt he won't be much longer now.

Jean.

Ah, well, that's all right, as long as I know what keeps him. Good morning. (*Hutton moves on.*) You see, mother, how they turn to Alan before all the rest!

Mrs. Holroyd.

Ah, well, when a lass is in love she must needs know better than her mother, I suppose.

Jean.

Ah, mother dear, wasn't there a time when you were a girl—when you knew better too?

Mrs. Holroyd.

(*shaking her head*) Eh, but that's a long time ago.

Jean.

But you remember it, I'll be bound! I think I'd best be setting that dish in the oven again; it will be getting cold. (*Exit with dish.*)

Mrs. Holroyd.

(*alone*) Well—(*shakes her head with a little smile as*

she goes on knitting)—there's nowt so queer as folk !
(*Shakes her head again.*)

Jean.

(*coming back*)   I wonder what makes him bide so
long ?

Mrs. Holroyd.

You had far better give over tewing, and sit
quietly down with a bit of work in your hands till
he comes.

Jean.

No, mother, I can't !   (*smiling*).   I'm too busy—
watching for him !   (*Leans over railing and looks
along road to the* R.)

Mrs. Holroyd.

That'll be Jamie coming along.   (*Looking off to
the* L.)

Jean.

(*looking round*) So it is. (*Indifferently*) Well,
Jamie, good morning. (*Warren, a small delicate
man, wearing a wide-awake hat and carrying a stick
in his hand, comes along the road from the* L.)

Warren.

Good morning, Jean.   Well, Mrs. Holroyd, how
are you ?

Jean.

(*Stands and leans against the railing to the* R, *looking
down the road and listening to what the others are
saying.*)

Mrs. Holroyd.

Good morning, my lad : sit down a bit.   And what
have you been doing the day ?   You look tired.

Warren.

(*takes off his hat wearily, passing his hand over his brow*) I've been doing my work—giving the Word to those who can hear it.

Mrs. Holroyd.

And you will have been edifying, that it will! And ye'll have done them good with it, for ye always were a beautiful speaker, Jamie!

Jean.

(*from the back*) Mother, I doubt you should call him Mr. Warren now he's a minister.

Mrs. Holroyd.

Eh, not I! I mind him since he was a bit of a lad running barefoot about the village at home.

Jean.

And do you mind, Jamie, that when you had a book in your hand I'd snatch it from you and throw it over the hedge? (*Laughs.*)

Warren.

Yes, you always pretended you didn't like books, Jean—but you used to learn quicker than anybody else when you chose.

Mrs. Holroyd.

And so she does still, I'm sure. She likes her book as well as any one, though she will have it that she doesn't. She'll sit and read to Alan, when he's smoking his pipe, for half an hour at a time.

Warren.

And what does he think of it?

Mrs. Holroyd.

(*smiling*) Between you and me, Jamie, I don't think he minds much for what she reads.

Jean.

(*hotly*) Indeed, but he does ! Alan can understand what I read just as well as me.

Mrs. Holroyd.

Eh, lass, it isn't the strongest in the arm that's the best at the books !

Warren.

Yes, it's rather hard upon the rest of us poor fellows if a fellow like Creyke is to have every-thing—if we mayn't have a little more book-learning to make up for not being a Hercules, like him.

Jean.

Why, Jamie, you wouldn't care to be a Hercules, as you call it—you never did.

Warren.

That's what you say.

Jean.

(*lightly, still watching road to the* R) Well, I say what I think, as honest folk do! (*Sheltering her eyes with her hand.*) Where can he be ? His dinner will be burnt to a cinder directly.

Mrs. Holroyd.

I wish he'd come and be done with it. She can't mind for anything else but yon dinner while she's waiting for him.

Warren.

Well, well, that's how it should be, I daresay.

Mrs. Holroyd.

And have you got settled in your new house against the chapel?

Warren.

Pretty well, yes.

Mrs. Holroyd.

Ah, I doubt you find it hard. A man's a poor creature at siding up, and getting things straight.

Warren.

He is indeed!

Mrs. Holroyd.

(*sympathetically*) You'll be lonesome at times, my lad, isn't it so?

Warren.

(*shakes his head*) Indeed I am!

Mrs. Holroyd.

Come, you must get yourself a little wife, and she'll make it nice and homely for you.

Warren.

(*shakes his head*) No, I don't think I shall be taking a wife yet a bit, somehow. (*Gets up.*) Well, I must be going. (*Looks at his watch.*) I said I would look in at the school for a bit after dinner, and the children go in again at half-past one.

Jean.

Yes, I always see them bustling past—some of them so little that if they didn't take hold of each other's hands they'd be tumbling down! (*She laughs.*)

Warren.

Yes, there are some very weeny ones in the infant school.   Canny little bairns !   Good-bye, Jean—good-bye, Mrs. Creyke.

Jean.

Good-bye, Jamie !   (*Exit Warren to the* R.)

Mrs. Holroyd.

Eh, but he has a tender heart.   I like a man that can speak about the little ones that way.

Jean.

So do I.   Oh, mother, I like to watch Alan with a child—the way he looks at it and the way he speaks to it !   Do you know, with those strong arms of his he can hold a baby as well as you, mother?   He picked up a little mite that was sobbing on the road the other day, and carried it home, and before a minute was over the bairn had left off crying, and nestled itself to sleep on his shoulder.

Mrs. Holroyd.

Ah, yes, he'll make a good father some day !

Jean.

A good father and a happy one, too !   Yes, we shall be happier then than we are now even.   Oh, mother, is that possible ?—shall I be happier when I have my baby in my arms?

Mrs. Holroyd.

Ah, my child, yes, you will that, in truth.   People talk of happiness and the things that bring it, and the young people talk about it and dream of it—but there's one happiness in the world that's better and bigger when it comes than one ever thinks for beforehand—and that is the moment when a woman's first child lies in her arms.

Jean.

Is it, is it really?   Oh, mother, to think that this is coming to me!   I shall have that too, besides all the rest!   Isn't it wonderful?

Mrs. Holroyd.

(*moved*)   God keep you, honey !

Jean.

Yes, when I think of the moment when my child will lie in my arms, how he will look at me——

Mrs. Holroyd.

(*smiling*)   *He !*   It's going to be a boy then, is it ?

Jean.

Of course it is!   Like his father.   He shall be called Alan, too, and he will be just like him.   He will have the same honest blue eyes, that make you believe in them, and the same yellow hair and a straight nose, and a firm, sweet mouth.   But that's what he'll be like when he grows up a little ; at first he'll be nothing but a pink, soft, round, little baby, and we will sit before the fire—it will be the winter, you know, when he comes—and he'll lie across my knee, and stretch out his little pink feet to the blaze, and all the neighbours will come in and see his sturdy little limbs, and say, " My word, what a fine boy ! "   He'll be just such another as his father. Oh, mother, it's too good to be true !

Mrs. Holroyd.

No, no, honey, it isn't !   It will all come true some day.

2

Jean.

Oh, mother, mother, what a good world it is!
(*kisses her*)   Ah, I see some more people coming—
he'll soon be here now! (*Goes in to* R.)

Mrs. Holroyd.

(*looking along road*) Yes, there they come. (*Gets
up, puts her knitting down, begins straightening table,
then goes in as though to fetch something.*)

(*Gradual signs of commotion, two boys rush along
stage from* R *to* L, *then return with two more, and go
off,* R.   *Two children rush past ; then two women enter
at back,* L, *and stand a little to the* R *of cottage, shading
their eyes.   Mrs. Holroyd comes out of door with a
brown jug in her hand.*)

Mrs. Holroyd.

What is it ?   Anything happened ?

1st Woman.

Ay, it's an accident, they say, at the works.

Mrs. Holroyd.

(*alarmed*)   An accident ?

2nd Woman.

Yes, yes, look there !   (*She points off to the* R.)

Jean.

(*leaning out of room to the* L, *with her arms crossed on
window sill*) And, mother, I've been thinking we
shall have to call him wee Alan, to tell him from his
father, you know.   Mother ! (*looks*) Mother, what
has happened ?

Mrs. Holroyd.

(*hurriedly*) Nothing, honey, nothing. (*Jean comes
hurriedly out of room and down passage.*)

Jean.

No, mother, I am sure there is something!
What is it. (*To woman*) Do you know?

1st Woman.

It will be an accident, they say, at the works.

Jean.

At the works! Any one hurt?

2nd Woman.

Eh, with yon machines, ye never know but there'll
be something.

Jean.

With the machines? (*Sees Warren coming hurriedly past*, R.) Jamie, Jamie, what is it? What
has happened?

Warren.

Jean, dear Jean, you must be prepared.

Jean.

Prepared? For what?

Warren.

There has been an accident.

Jean.

Not to Alan? Ah, do you mean he has been
hurt? (*Warren is silent.*) But he's so strong it
will be nothing! I'll make him well again. Where
is he? We must bring him back!

Warren.

No, no! (*He looks back at something approaching.*)

Jean.

What is that? (*Pause.*)

Warren.

God's will be done, Jean; His hand is heavy on ye. (*A moment of silence. Jean is seen to look aghast at something coming. Hutton and two more, carrying a covered litter, come to the gate, followed by a little crowd of men, women and children.*)

Jean.

Oh, they're coming here! (*Rushes to them.*) Hutton, tell me what has happened?

Hutton.

Best not look, missis—it's a sore sight! (*Mrs. Holroyd holds Jean back.*)

Jean.

Let me be, mother—I *must* go to him!

1st Woman.

Na, na, my lass—best keep back!

Mrs. Holroyd.

Keep back, honey! you're not the one to bear the sight!

Jean.

I *must*—let me go! (*Struggles, breaks away, and rushes forward—lifts up cover*) Alan! (*She falls back with a cry into Mrs. Holroyd's arms.*)

CURTAIN.

SCENE II.

A room in Jean's cottage. Fireplace to the R, with chimneypiece on which are candlesticks, tapers, etc.; door at back, L C. Window to L with curtains; kitchen dresser to L with plates, jugs, and a bowl with green spray in it. A mahogany bookcase on back wall, a table back C, chairs, etc. ; a cradle half way down the stage to the L of C.

> *(Jean discovered sitting listlessly by the fire. She is in a white gown with a black shawl over it. Mrs. Holroyd and Mrs. Ridley are standing one on each side of the cradle, Mrs. Holroyd bending over it, smoothing the clothes, etc., Mrs. Ridley standing by admiringly.)*

Mrs. Holroyd.

(L *of cradle, finishing tucking it up*) There now, he looks the picture of comfort, the dear ! and so sound asleep, it's a pleasure to see him.

Mrs. Ridley.

(*right of cradle, looking at him*) It is indeed ; but I doubt you've got him too hot, Mrs. Holroyd.

Mrs. Holroyd.

(*doubtfully*) Too hot, do you think so? Well, perhaps we might put off this quilt. (*Takes it off and stands with it in her hand*) And yet, I don't know, I am all for weeny babies being kept warm enough. (*Puts the quilt on again.*)

Mrs. Ridley.

Warm enough! Yes, but not stifled—ye'll fair smother the bairn with all yon clothes! (*Takes off quilt.*)

Mrs. Holroyd.

Ay, now, it's difficult to know what one should do for the best! (*Stands looking doubtfully at cradle.*)

Mrs. Ridley.

Well, I always say with a baby, you can't do better than take a neighbour's advice, and one that's had eleven too. My bairns used just to lie in the cot with a patchwork counterpane over them—it's a grand thing for a baby is the patchwork—and they grew up fine, sturdy lads as you'd wish to see.

Mrs. Holroyd.

Ah, fine and sturdy—that's just it! But it's very different with this poor little mite.

Mrs. Ridley.

(*her arms folded as she holds the quilt, shaking her head and looking compassionately at the baby*) Ay, poor wee thing, indeed! well, the Lord's will be done! He must have His own way with the bairns, as with everything else.

Mrs. Holroyd.

Do you know, I think I'll leave the quilt on.

(*takes it*)   I am fearful of the draughts down the chimney coming to him.

Mrs. Ridley.

Eh, yes—every chimney 'll blow both hot and cold, as the saying is.   I'm all for keeping the fresh air from a baby till he's turned the twelvemonth. Eh, but his mother should see him now, looking so fine and comfortable! (*looking round at Jean.   Jean pays no attention*)   Jean, he's looking as happy as a prince, the dear!   (*Jean is absorbed in thought.*)

Mrs. Holroyd.

(*shakes her head.   Half aside to Mrs. Ridley*)   Ah, it's not much his mother wants to see him, I'm afraid.   Jean!

Jean.

(*as though waking out of a reverie*)   Yes, mother, what is it?   (*Sits up.*)

Mrs. Holroyd.

The baby has gone to sleep—he's quite comfortable now.

Jean.

Asleep, is he?   Yes.   (*Leans forward, her head on her right hand, her elbow on her knee.   Mrs. Holroyd puts her hand down to the ground near the cradle.*)

Mrs. Holroyd.

I thought I felt a bit of a draught here, near the cradle head.

Mrs. Ridley.

(*putting her hand to the ground with an anxious look*) No, no!   There's no draught; it's just yourself that's made it, whisking round with your petticoats.

Mrs. Holroyd.

Well, happen you're right. (*Holds her skirts carefully together, then feels for the draught again*) Na, na, there's no draught here. He'll sleep now, right enough.

Mrs. Ridley.

If he does it'll be more by good luck than good management, with all yon clothes on the top of him!

Mrs. Holroyd.

He should—he's not had much sleep this day, nor last night either.

Mrs. Ridley.

And you look tired with it, Mrs. Holroyd.

Mrs. Holroyd.

We've had a restless day with him, haven't we, Jean?

Jean.

(*indifferently*) Yes, he's cried.

Mrs. Ridley.

It's too much for you, Mrs. Holroyd, to have been after that bairn ever since daylight.

Mrs. Holroyd.

Eh well! It's my Jean's bairn, you know.

Mrs. Ridley.

Yes, that's just it! It's Jean's bairn, and it's Jean ought to be tewing with it—it would do her good, Mrs. Holroyd.

Mrs. Holroyd.

Eh, I doubt she's not strong enough yet! But you are right: she should take an interest in it, all the same. I can't get her to seem as though she minded for it, do what I will.

Mrs. Ridley.

You should rouse her a bit, and not let her sit mounging that way. (*Cheerily*) Come, Jean, do you think the cradle is out of the draught there, or shall we get it moved a bit?

Jean.

(*half looking round, then subsides again*) Oh, I think it will do very well where it is.

Mrs. Holroyd.

Ah, honey, I don't like to see you sitting there as though you had nothing to do with the bairn.

Jean.

Nay, mother, I know it's well cared for with you looking after it—and Mrs. Ridley.

Mrs. Holroyd.

Ah, but that's not enough. Ah, Jean, how little I thought when you used to talk of your baby, and long to have it in your arms, that you would be so hard to the little fatherless child when it came, and not bear to look at it, just because it isn't the fine lusty lad you wanted! (*Jean shudders as she sits and looks into the fire. Mrs. Holroyd is bustling about, arranging the room as she talks.*)

Mrs. Ridley.

Yes, poor wee thing! He can't help being a cripple; you should care for him all the more because he won't walk and run like other boys. What's a mother for, if it's not to care for the bairn that needs it most?

Jean.

(*looks into the fire*) Yes, yes, I suppose so ! that is what's left—there'll be nothing else in my life.

Mrs. Holroyd.

Nothing else ! You ought to be thankful for having the child !

Jean.

(*bitterly*) Thankful !

Mrs. Ridley.

Ah, Jean, I doubt you have a hard heart ! You don't know the blessings you have.

Jean.

(*covers her face, then goes on after a minute*) No, maybe I don't. Do you remember, mother, that last afternoon that we talked about the child that was to come? You told me how beautiful everything would be, and that I should be happier than ever I'd been before. Happier—ah !

Mrs. Holroyd.

It's not ours to tell the future, and it's very wicked to repine when things are not as we hoped.

Jean.

(*half to herself—looking into the fire*) I used to hope, all those happy weeks before that day, and then afterwards, when my only hope was in the bairn—and now I have no hope left . . . only horrible certainty !

Mrs. Holroyd.

Eh, Jean, yours is sinful talk—you must just be a good mother to the bairn now that it is here (*arranging room*).

Mrs. Ridley.

(*Kneeling in front of fire, takes up fire-irons in her hand, and sweeps hearth.*) Ay, there's many a mother with a family of fine boys and girls has thought more of her one deformed child than all the rest !

Jean.

(*covering her face*) Deformed ! Yes, that's what they'll call him. (*Pause.*)

Mrs. Ridley.

Why, there's Meg Dowden who used to live beside the Green at home—how she used to go about with that little Tommy of hers, who could only sling along the road instead of walking ! and she was as proud of him as you please. Then there's Kate Lockerby, when one of her bairns wasn't right in her head——

Jean.

Don't ! Don't ! I can't bear it !

Mrs. Ridley.

Ah well, child, you must try to bear it, and to put up with things that can't be mended.

Mrs. Holroyd.

Yes, honey, you must put off that hard, rebellious spirit, and put on a meek and submissive one, else you will be punished for your pride some day. (*Goes on dusting and arranging room, etc.*)

Mrs. Ridley.

Ah, but a young thing like that will feel it ! I mind when my Johnnie was born, that only lived a week——

Jean.

Don't tell me about it, I say, don't tell me about any other woman's child !

Mrs. Ridley.

My word, Jean, but you've got your saucy tongue in your head still ! I'll tell you what, Mrs. Holroyd, you ought to have the minister to her when she speaks that way; he would bring her to a better way of thinking.

Mrs. Holroyd.

(*aside to Mrs. Ridley*) I've told him to-day just to step in and see her. Ye see, Mrs. Ridley, when the lass has been about a bit longer, she'll be better ; she hasn't got her strength yet.

Mrs. Ridley.

Ay, that's true—any one can see that to look at her. She's as white as a sheet to-night.

Mrs. Holroyd.

Indeed, she is that ! Come, dearie, get to bed with you, and you'll feel better in the morning.

Jean.

(*wearily*) To bed—very well !

Mrs. Holroyd.

Everything is ready for you in the next room— and Mrs. Ridley will sit here and be a bit of company for you while I go back home to see how things are going on.

Mrs. Ridley.

Eh, that I will. I'll sit here as long as you please. (*Sits by table to the* L *Gets out her knitting.*)

Jean.

No, no! I don't want any one to stay with me.

Mrs. Ridley.

Eh, I can knit just as well here as at home. My boys are on the night shift this week, and won't be in for supper.

Mrs. Holroyd.

(*to Mrs. Ridley*) And if the baby cries you can just put it over again.

Mrs. Ridley.

No need to tell me what to do with a baby, that's had eleven to look after ; and I can do for Jean too, if she wants anything.

Jean.

No, no; I can quite well fend for myself. I sha'n't want anything.

Mrs. Holroyd.

(*anxiously*) But what about the baby? I doubt you won't be able to manage him, Jean?

Jean.

Yes, yes, I shall! Didn't you say that's what a mother's for? (*Mrs. Ridley gets up.*)

Mrs. Ridley.

(*to Mrs. Holroyd*) Well, neighbour, I believe the lass is right ; and if you take my advice, you'll do as she says, and leave her to tew with the baby ; she'll soonest get to care for him that way.

Mrs. Holroyd.

Maybe you are right after all.

Mrs. Ridley.

Well, if I'm not wanted then, I'd best be getting

home.   Good night to you !   (*Shakes her head to herself as she goes out*)   Eh, but some folks are bad to do with when they're in trouble !   (*Exit.*)

Jean.

You go too, mother ; I shall be all right.

Mrs. Holroyd.

Suppose you wanted anything, or the baby wasn't well ?

Jean.

Well, if the worst came to the worst, I could step up so far and fetch you : it's only a few doors off.

Mrs. Holroyd.

Yes ; you could do that after all.   Good night, then, honey !   Go to bed, say your prayers, and wake up stronger and better in the morning.   All that comes to us is for the best, you know, if we can but see it.

Jean.

Good night !   (*Her mother kisses her.   Mrs. Holroyd goes out, after giving a last look at the baby, and a general straightening touch to things as she passes.*) At last !   Oh, if they would only give over telling me it's for the best !   (*Looks at cradle*)   For the best !   *That* for the best !   (*Bends over cradle*)   But he has got a darling little face all the same !   Poor little bairn—my poor little bairn !   They say I don't love you—I don't care for you at all !   Yes, yes, I do, dear, yes, I do !   (*Buries her face and sobs. Knock heard at the door.   Gets up, drying her eyes, and stands at foot of cradle, looking at child.   Jean looks round, crosses to fire—another knock.*)   Yes ? who is it ?   (*Warren on the threshold.*)

Warren.

Good evening, Jean! (*Pause—Jean still looking into fire—Warren stands hesitating, and a little embarrassed at her inhospitality*) Your mother asked me to look in, and——

Jean.

And tell me of my sinful ways—yes, I know! Come in, Jamie!

Warren.

(*comes forward*) Jean, how ill you look! You're fretting; you mustn't rebel so against the visitation o' God! His laws are——

Jean.

Good and merciful. Yes, I've heard that!

Warren.

Eh! I hope you're not doubting His loving-kindness, Jean!

Jean.

I'm not thinking about God, nor about loving-kindness.

Warren.

But you must, child. It'll steady and strengthen ye. Ye'll find His mercy everywhere.

Jean.

Do you think I'll find it in the cradle, yon?

Warren.

Eh? (*shaking his head*) Yes, I know what you mean. I've heard——

Jean.

(*with smothered anguish, breaking in*) Then you forgot, Jamie Warren, or you wouldn't talk of loving-kindness. You forgot God couldn't even take Alan away without—without—— (*covers her face and shudders.*)

Warren.

Jean! You're tempting the Almighty!

Jean.

Ye hadn't heard, maybe, that a little child was sent, hideous and maimed, to stumble through this terrible world—eh?

Warren.

Hush, hush, my girl! You're ill, or you wouldn't talk that wild and wicked way! (*As Jean is about to break in*) When you're stronger you'll see how the child'll comfort you.

Jean.

(*slowly*) But how shall I comfort the child?

Warren.

He'll grow up to be a scholar and a God-fearing man yet, Jean. It's no ill fate.

Jean.

He'll grow up, you think?

Warren.

(*cheerily*) Aye, why not? He may quite well live to be old.

Jean.

You don't think that? (*seizes Warren by the arm.*)

Warren.

Of course. Why not? He's not rightly formed, poor bairn, else he's sturdy enough, they say. He may outlive us all, yet!

Jean.

You think he'll live longer than any of us?
(*hoarsely*).

Warren.

Well, in the course of nature and if God wills it ;
(*Jean turns away*) but if it's the will of God that the
child should be taken, Jean, you must bow to His
will.

Jean.

You're sure the bairn would go to heaven, Jamie?

Warren.

How can you doubt it? Ye'll be having him
baptised ?

Jean.

Baptised ! (*listlessly*) Yes, I suppose so.

Warren.

Ah, Jean, take care lest it be too late ! i The
innocent bairn mustn't suffer for the sinful neglect of
others. Unless he be baptised, who can be sure?
Jean, see to it that the child is saved.

Jean.

Saved ! Why was he not saved from *that* ?

Warren.

We are not here to ask that. It is enough for us
to know that it is the will of God.

Jean.

(*passionately*) The will of God ! I won't believe it !

Warren.

Jean !

Jean.

Or if you're right, so much the worse, then ! If

3

God were full of mercy and loving-kindness as you
say, how could He be so cruel to a little harmless
child? (*crosses to cradle, and drops on her knees
beside it*).

Warren.

Jean, Jean, ye tempt the Almighty by your wicked
words. But I doubt you're sore at heart. His mercy
endureth for ever; He will forgive you, and He'll
have pity on you.

Jean.

(*with a burst of agony*) Pity on *me*, man! It's the
child! It's the *child!* Don't you think I'd be glad
to give up my health and strength to my baby? If
God was angry at *me*, why didn't He strike *me*
down? If I'd been doing wrong, He should have
cursed *me*, and not hurt Alan's little bairn! *I* could
have borne it. This minute I could stand up and
let them hack me all to pieces if they'd make my
baby straight and strong. (*Jean walks unsteadily
back towards fireplace.*)

Warren.

Hush! hush! You'll come to better reason as the
time goes on, (*Jean absorbed in her grief*) if you'll
but strive in prayer to be given a meek spirit, and
strength to bear your burden bravely, Jean. There's
many a one has had to go through the world before
bearing a cross as heavy as yours.

Jean.

And does it make it any better for me to think of
those other wretched women?

Warren.

Ah, Jean, seek for strength where alone it can be

found—pray for it, only pray, and it shall be given you! (*Jean stands looking at the fire trying to control herself.*) (*Moved*) Jean, my poor Jean, good-bye! I'll pray for you and for the bairn—I'll pray that God may bring you peace. (*Exit.*)

Jean.

(*alone—wildly*) Pray for the bairn—pray, pray! (*she falls on her knees*) Oh God! If I've been wicked, don't make it worse for the child—punish me some other way—don't hurt him any more—he's so little, dear God—so helpless, and he never did any wrong! *He* hasn't been drunk with life and strength and love—he hasn't walked through the world exulting and fearless and forgetting You. That was I, oh, Father in heaven! Punish *me*—and take the baby away. This is a hard place—this world down here. Take him away! Take him away! (*She staggers to her feet—listens*) He is stirring. (*Goes and looks in cradle—leans over it*) Ah, how little you must know to be smiling in your sleep! (*Drops on her knees by the cradle*) Dear little face! Ah! It's brave of you to smile when God has laid such heavy burdens on you! Do you think you will be able to smile later on when you see other boys running and leaping and being glad—when you're a man, dear, and see how good it is to be strong and fair? Can you bear it, little one? (*She rocks the cradle as if to hush him, though the child sleeps on—she croons drearily*) Never mind, never mind! Mother'll be always at your side—always—always. (*She stops, horror-stricken*) Always? Who can say so? I might die! It's natural I should go first and leave him to the mercy of——Oh, I cannot, I cannot! I *dare* not! (*Bows her head over the cradle's edge— then half recovering, and yet with suppressed wildness, whispers*) Baby, I'm frightened! Listen, I don't know what to do. Do you *want* to live? Tell me, shall you ever hate me for this horrible gift of life? (*With wide vacant eyes*) Oh, I seem to see you in some far-off time, your face distorted like your body, but with bitterness and loathing, saying, "Mother, how *could* you be so cruel as to let me live and suffer? You could have eased my pain; you could have saved me this long martyrdom; when I was little and lay in your arms. Why didn't you save me. You were a coward—a coward!" (*She bows her head over the cradle again, overcome—then she lifts a drawn white face*) It would be quite easy—only to cover the dear face a little while—only to shut out the air and light for a little while, and remember I'm fighting for his release. Yes, it would be quite easy—if only one's heart didn't sink and one's brain grow numb! (*Leans against the cradle, faint—her eyes fall on the child*) Are your lips moving, dear? (*Pause*) Are you asking for life? No, you don't want to live, do you? No, no, you cannot! Darling, it will be so easy—you'll never know—it will only be that you'll go on sleeping—sleeping, until you wake up in heaven! (*Clutches quilt together quickly, then stops*) In heaven! No—what did Jamie say? "Unless he be baptised"—(*stands a minute—repeats to herself*) He said, "See to it that the child is saved." Yes, darling, that's what I'm trying to do to save you! (*Lets quilt fall—stands staring into space—moves like a woman in a dream; brings two candles; returns,*

*brings a bowl of water, and a big book with silver
clasps; puts all on table by cradle—lights candles—
lifts the great book, and goes to the cradle and looks at
the child—turns away with a sob, and, standing by
the candle-light, opens the book and tries to find the
place—passes her hand across her eyes.)* Where is the
place? I can't find it! I can't find it! *(Tries again
—then falls on her knees between the table and the
cradle—she closes the great book and whispers)* Have
pity on us, Lord—show us the way! *(Still on her
knees, she lets the book fall to the floor, dips her hand
in the water and sprinkles the child)* I baptise thee,
Alan! *(Prays a moment—then stands looking yearn-
ingly at him)* Alan, my little Alan! *Rises—looks
anxiously over her shoulder to door and window, blows
out the candles one by one, and goes stealthily towards
cradle with a long wailing cry, the eider quilt hugged
to her breast as the*

CURTAIN FALLS.

SCENE III.

Room in the prison.

(Colonel Stuart sitting at writing-table with papers to the R. *Chief warder standing by him. Door* C. *Door to the* L.)

Col. Stuart.

You have nothing more to report, Roberts?

Roberts.

No, sir ; nothing.

Col. Stuart.

And Jean Creyke ?

Roberts.

Just the same, sir. Can get nothing out of her.

Col. Stuart.

(shaking his head) Ah ! Well, you can take these. *(Gives him papers. Roberts gathers up papers and is turning away. Enter a Warder at* C.)

Warder.

Please, sir, there is some one to see the woman Creyke.

Col. Stuart.

Who is it ?

Warder.

An old woman, sir, of the name of Holroyd.   She
is Creyke's mother, I believe.

Col. Stuart.

Her mother ?   Bring her in here.   (*Exit Warder.*)
I can't help feeling that there must be some extenu-
ating circumstance if only we could get at it.

Roberts.

Well, sir, maybe there is.   It's a bad business,
anyway!   (*Salutes, and goes out with papers at door* L.
Enter Mrs. Holroyd with Warder.   Exit Warder.)

Col. Stuart.

Mrs. Holroyd ?

Mrs. Holroyd.

(*with her handkerchief to her eyes*)   Ay, yes, your
worship, my name is Holroyd.

Col. Stuart.

(*kindly*)   I am very sorry for you ; it must be a hard
trial.

Mrs. Holroyd.

Ah, it's hard indeed to think that a girl of mine
should have taken her own child's life.

Col. Stuart.

Yes, it's a very terrible story.   (*Pause.*)

Mrs. Holroyd.

(*anxiously*)   What will they do to her, your worship ?
(*Col. Stuart is silent.*)   They won't take her life, will
they ?   There must be a chance for her yet.

Col. Stuart.

I fear not much ; a reprieve has been asked for,
but——

Mrs. Holroyd.

Yes, I know—Jamie Warren said he would bring the news this morning, the moment it was known.

Col. Stuart.

Jamie Warren?

Mrs. Holroyd.

Yes ; he's the minister down at our place ; he's always been a good friend to our Jean, and if she would have listened to him, and not taken up with Creyke, things would have been very different.

Col. Stuart.

Well, there seems to be very little here to found an appeal for mercy on. We know so little of the whole thing. What could have made her kill the child? Do you think her mind was at all affected at the time ?

Mrs. Holroyd.

Her mind! My Jean's? No, indeed! Why did she kill the little baby ? Well, it was a poor wreckling, the lamb, and it well-nigh broke her heart that it wasn't fine and sturdy like the father, —she wanted a boy like the husband she lost—she never seemed to take to the baby, never from the first, and she never would tew with it as mothers do.

Col. Stuart.

Do you mean that that's why she killed the poor little helpless child—that she could find it in her heart to kill it because it wasn't strong and sturdy ?

Mrs. Holroyd.

Ah, yes, your worship, it's hard my Jean should have done it. I well-nigh can't believe it of my own bairn.

Col. Stuart.

It's hard to believe of any mother.

Mrs. Holroyd.

And if they spare her life what will become of her? Can I have her back with me to her home again?

Col. Stuart.

No, my poor woman, she can't go back to you again. The best will be that her sentence will be commuted to penal servitude for life.

Mrs. Holroyd.

(*crying out*) For life! My Jean? Oh Lord, oh Lord, Your hand is heavy on us!

Col. Stuart.

You shall see her. (*Rings bell.*) (*A Warder comes in*) Jean Creyke is to come here. (*Exit Warder.*) (*To Mrs. Holroyd*) Perhaps you can bring her to a better frame of mind. She seems strangely hardened.

Mrs. Holroyd.

Ah, your worship, I am afraid she won't mind for me; she always knew I hadn't the wits to be up to her, or find the words to say to her. Oh, my poor girl, she always was too proud, I always told her she was. The Lord has punished her. (*Enter Jean with two Warders.*)

Mrs. Holroyd.

Oh, Jean, Jean! (*Jean's sentences are given as a stage direction of what she is silently to convey, but she does not speak until nearly the end of the Act.*)

Jean.

(*silent*) Mother!

Mrs. Holroyd.

Honey, tell his worship how you came to do it.
Tell him you hadn't your wits right ; that you didn't
know what you were doing to the little bairn !

Jean.

(*silent*)   I knew well enough.

Mrs. Holroyd.

Oh, my dear, if you could tell him something that
would make them let you off—now think, Jean,
think, honey ! it may be you could tell them something that would save you.

Jean.

(*silent—stares vacantly into space*)   I can tell him
nothing.

Col. Stuart.

Nothing you can say, of course, will clear you
now ; but, for the sake of the memory you will leave
behind you, can you give no sort of reason, no
explanation of the impulse that led to your terrible
crime ?   (*Jean shakes her head.*)

Mrs. Holroyd.

Oh, your worship, your worship !

Col. Stuart.

(*to Mrs. Holroyd*)   No, it is no use, I'm afraid ; she
hasn't opened her lips from the beginning. (*Looks at
watch*)   You have twenty minutes together. (*Exit.*)
(*The two Warders stand at the back, apparently not
listening.*)

Mrs. Holroyd.

(*in tears*)   Oh, my Jean, my bonny Jean ! That it
should have come to this ! (*Jean stands motionless.*

Mrs. Holroyd turns away, distractedly wringing her hands.)

Mrs. Holroyd.

(*coming back to the girl*) Jean, Jean, do you know they will have the life of ye ?

Jean.

(*silent. Makes motion of assent*) Yes, I know.

Mrs. Holroyd.

How could you do it, my lass? Can't you remember? If you could have told them all about it and asked for mercy you could have got it.

Jean.

(*silent—smiles strangely*) I don't want mercy.

Mrs. Holroyd.

You're not afraid to die with your sins about ye?

Jean.

(*silent—shakes her head*) No, I am not afraid.

Mrs. Holroyd.

Ah, Jean, but I am afraid for ye. No, I cannot bear it. Jean! (*with a fresh outburst*) Are ye not thinking of your mother at all?

Jean.

(*silent—puts out her hand to her mother*) Poor mother!

Mrs. Holroyd.

Oh, Jean, you're very hard. You don't think of those who are left when you won't ask for mercy. And Jamie Warren, poor lad—his heart is broken as well as mine. (*Pause—Jean stands erect seeming not to hear.*) But there is still a chance, Jean—honey

—there is indeed.   Maybe Jamie 'll come back here
this morning with the blessed news.   He should be
here soon, very soon.   (*In an agony*)   Jean, Jean, if
only I could get you to speak!   His worship's been
asking me about you.   What can I tell him?   Try
to recollect, lassie—try to think on that night, when I
left ye with the baby—try to think just how it all
was.   I left ye sitting by the fire, just after Mrs.
Ridley had gone out; ye'll mind she was a bit vexed,
poor body, at the way ye'd spoken—and the baby
was asleep in the cradle, I'd just covered him up
warm with the quilt.   (*Jean gives a sharp cry, and
makes a motion to stop her mother.*)

Jean.

(*silent*)   Ah!   (*The door opens, and James Warren
comes in hastily with a Warder, who points to Jean
and goes out again.*)

Mrs. Holroyd.

Jamie!   Well, Jamie—what news do you bring?
Speak, lad, tell us!

Warren.

(*looks at Mrs. Holroyd and shakes his head, and then
looks at Jean.*)   The news I bring is—bad.

Jean.

(*silent—unmoved*)

Warren.

No, Jean, they won't grant it; they say the sentence must be carried out.   (*Jean clasps her hands
with a look of relief, almost of gladness.*)

Mrs. Holroyd.

Oh, Jean, honey, it will kill me too!   (*Jean seems

not to hear.) Jamie, Jamie, she doesn't seem to mind for me one little bit! Speak to her, my lad, try to soften her hard heart! (*Re-enter Col. Stuart.*)

Col. Stuart.
(*to Jean*)　You have heard the result of the appeal?

Jean.
(*silent—bows.*)　Yes.

Mrs. Holroyd.
Oh, your worship, is there no hope?

Col. Stuart.
None—absolutely none.

Warren.
Jean, your only hope is in Him who alone can pardon your sin : turn to Him before it is too late. Do not die unforgiven.

Jean.
(*silent*)　I shall not die unforgiven.

Col. Stuart.
Take care, Jean Creyke ; remember your time is running short—the end is very near.

Jean.
(*aloud*)　When?

Col. Stuart.
To-morrow morning at eight.

Jean.
To-morrow!　(*Her lips form the word.*)

Mrs. Holroyd.
(*crying out*)　To-morrow morning!

Warren.

Yes, the time is short, indeed! Jean, confess!
Confess, and turn you to the Lord your God.

Mrs. Holroyd.

To-morrow! To-morrow! Ah, but it's too
soon for her to die! Jean, Jean, my honey, my
little lass! Oh, my Jean! (*Jean, as if in a dream,
turns to go.*)

Col. Stuart.

My poor woman, all you can do for her now is
to pray for her, and say good-bye. You won't see
her again.

Mrs. Holroyd.

(*horror-stricken and bewildered*) Not see her again!
What do you mean? You'll let me come to-night,
and to-morrow? (*Looks round—reads answer in
faces of bystanders.*)

Col. Stuart.

No, this is the last time.

Mrs. Holroyd.

The last time! No, no! You can't take her
from me like that! Your worship, she's the only
child I've ever had—the only thing I have in the
world! Eh, but ye'll let me bide with her the day,
till to-night, only till to-night! Just these few hours
longer! Think, your worship—I must do without
her all the rest of my life!

Col. Stuart.

(*compassionately*) My poor woman! (*He makes a
sign to the warders.*)

Mrs. Holroyd.

(*rushing forward as Warders are going to take Jean
out*) Oh, wait, only wait! Jamie, don't let her go!
Tell them they mustn't take her to die yet. She
isn't ready to die, ye know she isn't ready. (*To Jean*)
Oh, my honey! Speak, speak, before it is too late.
Tell them why you did it. Put away your rebellious
heart! (*To Stuart*) You think she's bad and
wicked, but she's not wicked—she's not indeed!
Jean, Jean, why did ye kill the poor little bairn?

Warren.

Jean, listen to me—to-morrow you are to appear
before your Maker. Confess your crime, and lay
down your burden before the throne of God.

Jean.

(*aloud*) Crime!

Col. Stuart.

Not a crime, that you in cold blood took the life
of a poor, helpless, little 'baby, because you hadn't
the courage to bear the sight of its misfortunes?

Jean.

I hadn't courage? I've had courage just once
in my life—just once in my life I've been strong and
kind—and it was the night I killed my child! (*She
turns away to door.*)

Warren.

Jean! (*Mrs. Holroyd cries something inarticulate
as she tries in despair to hold Jean back.*)

Jean.

Don't, mother, don't! You don't think I could
live after this, do you? I had to do what I did,

and they have to take my life for it. I showed him the only true mercy, and that is what the law shows me! Maybe I shall find him up yonder made straight and fair and happy—find him in Alan's arms. Good-bye—mother—goodbye!

(She goes out as)

CURTAIN FALLS.

Appendix I.

(*a*) Extract from article signed " A. B. W." in *The Speaker*, May 6th, 1893 :—

" It is a philosophical commonplace that nature is, in some aspects, unjust, immoral, malignant, ferocious, 'red in tooth and claw.' Life presents us occasionally with cases of unspeakable calamity for which there can be no compensation ; wrongs that can never be righted ; hopeless, heartless, odious things which put the glib commonplaces of the pulpit and the copybook to the rout, and leave poor, mocked mankind shaking their fists in impotent rage at the sky. I read the other day in a newspaper of two women whom a recent shipwreck had not only made widows but driven—through the prolonged agony of hoping for tidings of the lost vessel which were never to arrive—raving mad. Are there not scores of instances on record of people done to death by the law whose innocence has been clearly established—too late ? Take another case. A young bride, idolising her husband, glorying in his strength and shapeliness, has him brought home to her on a stretcher, an unrecognisable mass of mangled flesh and crushed bones. That, you admit, is an awful calamity, but time, you hasten to add, will bring its anodyne ; the woman is herself young and strong, she will outlive her trouble, there is yet a reasonable prospect of a decent, happy life in store for her. But, suppose, further, that a baby is born to her, a baby which will for its whole life bear perpetual witness to the shock its mother had undergone—weak, deformed to hideousness. Here you have, I think, one of those terrible cases which seem to be absolutely without consolation or redress. It is the case which has been presented at the Independent

4

Theatre by the anonymous author of *Alan's Wife*, and presented with no attenuation but rather persistent aggravations of its horrible circumstances. We are shown the stretcher, the mangled corpse, the child."

(*b*) Portion of letter addressed to the Editor of *The Speaker*, and published May 13th, 1893.

" Sir,—In remonstrating with ' A. B. W.' upon his attitude towards *Alan's Wife*, I am anxious to make it clear from the outset that it is not his method of criticism that I call in question. His method, if not the only right one, is at least perfectly legitimate. A work of art—or, if that begs the question, a theatrical production—causes in him a certain overplus of disagreeable sensation ; whereupon he calls all his æsthetic gods to witness that he was bound by the eternal laws of art to feel as he did, and that whoever feels otherwise must be a person of inferior sensibility and brutish taste. This, I repeat, is legitimate enough.   Mr. Walkley is absolutely justified in trying to mould æsthetic law into harmony with his feeling, instead of trying, like the hodmen of criticism, to bring his feeling, or lack of feeling, into harmony with a half-understood hard-and-fast æsthetic law.   I have not even any hope of modifying Mr. Walkley's instinctive impression. All I would suggest is that those who feel otherwise may take heart of grace, and cherish a tremulous hope that the law and the prophets are not quite so solid on Mr. Walkley's side as he has argued himself into believing.

" There is one very curious point in his article of last week which shows how chary we should be of attributing bad faith to opponents in controversy.   Of course, there cannot be the remotest doubt of Mr. Walkley's good faith, of his desire to write fairly and truthfully ; yet he makes one statement of fact which, in a critic less obviously above suspicion, one would be apt to call deliberately misleading. ' We are shown,' he says, ' the stretcher, *the mangled corpse, the child.*'   Who can fail to understand from this that the mangled corpse and the hideously deformed baby are actually presented to the physical eyes of the audience ?   Note, please, that Mr. Walkley cannot declare the whole sentence to be figurative.   The stretcher is *not* figurative—we *do* see the harmless, necessary stretcher.

Moreover we see the cradle—a solid oak cradle, transparent, like the solid earth itself, to the eye of the imagination, but certainly not to the physical vision. If Mr. Walkley, with the 'red and rolling eye of imagination,' saw the mangled corpse under the plaid which covered the stretcher, and descried the deformed baby through the half-inch boards of the cradle, he thereby rendered conclusive, though involuntary, testimony to the art of the author, which he declares in the same breath to be non-existent. For, as a matter of fact, there were no mangled remains, there was no crippled child. I believe there was a man on the stretcher, simply because a man is a more convenient 'property' than a lay figure; but as no square inch of his anatomy was for a moment visible to the audience, any bundle of clothes would practically have done just as well. What was in the cradle I do not know—very probably nothing but bedclothes, for no soul among the audience could possibly see into it. I think Mr. Walkley will admit, on reflection, that he showed less than his usual lucidity in mixing up physical fact (the stretcher) with hallucination (the body and the baby) and treating them, so to speak, on the same plane.

"'But the impression was just as horrible,' Mr. Walkley objects, 'as if the gory body and the distorted child had actually been visible; so that it really mattered nothing whether they were or not.' Excuse me, it mattered every-thing. It meant all the difference between imaginative art and brainless brutality. In the first place, Mr. Walkley must know in his heart that the impression was *not* so horrible as if the reality, or a mechanical imitation of the reality, had been presented to the eye. The author might have borrowed mangled limbs from a dissecting-room, a crooked baby from Seven Dials, and exhibited them on the stage. This would not have been art, and would have merited the hisses of the audience, if not the interference of the police. The author did nothing of the sort. By the exercise of his imagination, excellently seconded by that of the actors, he worked upon Mr. Walkley's imagination until that sanest of critics apparently did not know what he saw and what he did not see. There was no obtruding of physical horror upon the physical senses; there was simply an appeal of mind to mind—in other words, there was art. We cannot all of us

love all forms of art, and no one can think the worse of Mr.
Walkley for disliking and deprecating this particular form.
But when he tries to make out that there is no difference
between the brutal physical obtrusion and the skilful mental
suggestion of horror, he does so at the risk of his reputation
as a thinker.

*   *   *   *   *

"WILLIAM ARCHER."

(*c*) Extract from an article signed "A. B. W."
in *The Speaker* of May 20th, 1893.

"As regards the letter of friendly remonstrance in last
week's *Speaker*, which my attitude towards *Alan's Wife* has
provoked from Mr. William Archer, he must excuse me if I
decline to let him lure me into the arena of critical controversy
over this painful work. To him a play which shows us a
mother murdering (before our eyes) her child, which has been
born deformed, because her husband has been seen by her
(and us) brought in on a stretcher, crushed to death, is a work
of art ; to me it is not, and there—Sarceyism or no Sarceyism
—I must leave it. But there is a question of fact to which
I am bound to refer. I said that the play showed us 'the
stretcher, the mangled corpse, the child.' Mr. Archer denies
the mangled corpse, and the child. Of the man on the
stretcher, he says that 'no square inch of his anatomy was for
a moment visible to the audience.' Here it is he who is
strangely mistaken, not I. The sheet was lifted by the wife
from the man's head and shoulders, which were streaked with
paint to indicate some hideous disfigurement. This I saw—
'*ce qu'on appelle vu, de mes yeux vu*'—and so did my neighbour
in the stalls. As to the child, Mr. Archer contends that we
were not 'shown' it, because it was in a cradle, which contained 'very probably nothing but bedclothes.' This is,
surely, a quibble. My meaning was plain : something that
purported to be a child (I learn that it was actually a doll),
something which the mother went through the performance
of smothering as the curtain descended, was brought on the
stage. The statement which Mr. Archer thinks misleading
was, I submit, absolutely truthful."

Alan's Wife.   53

(*d*) Letter, with enclosures, addressed to the Editor of *The Speaker*, and published, May 27th, 1893 :—

" Sir,—The last paragraph of ' A. B. W.'s ' last article does more to justify his horror of horrors than whole columns of argument. I have sometimes suspected his attitude on this question of being, in part, a harmless and unconscious affectation ; but I see I was quite wrong. No wonder Mr. Walkley finds such a play as *Alan's Wife* intolerable, for horror, however delicately handled, evidently begets in him a state of positive hallucination and makes him ' see red.' ' The sheet,' he avers, ' was lifted from the man's head and shoulders, which were streaked with paint to indicate some hideous disfigurement. This I saw—" *ce qu'on appelle vu, de mes yeux vu.*" ' That Mr. Walkley is telling the truth as to his subjective impression I don't for a moment doubt ; but the subjoined letters will, I think, make it abundantly clear that Mr. Walkley's impression does not correspond with the objective reality. He may possibly have caught a momentary glimpse of the man's head, though it was not the intention of either author or actress that any portion of the ' corpse ' should be visible ; but he certainly did not ' see ' (except in the subjective sense) any ' streaks of paint,' or other indications of ' hideous disfigurement,' for the very sufficient reason that there were none to see. I submit, then, that his statement is a curious and valuable document in the psychology of æsthetics, proving that artistic ' suggestion ' may, in certain cases, go the length of producing mesmeric or hypnotic illusion. Mr. Walkley suggests that I ' quibbled ' on the question of the child. He stated that he ' was shown ' a baby, and that baby, by direct implication, hideously deformed. It now appears that he saw no baby, straight or crooked, but only a cradle in which he was asked to imagine that a baby lay. It actually contained a doll ; but as Mr. Walkley does not profess that he saw the doll, and as I can positively affirm that no member of the audience could possibly see it, that fact is neither here nor there. My point is that Mr. Walkley's statement was calculated to convey to the mind of the reader that he actually saw a deformed baby, or something representing one, whereas there was nothing of the sort to be seen. Is it a quibble to maintain that sane criticism should draw a sharp distinction between what is presented to the eye and what is merely suggested to the imagination ? Your obedient servant,

"WILLIAM ARCHER."

[ENCLOSURES.]

" DEAR MR. ARCHER,—It is possible that, in the excitement of the moment, I may have raised the covering so far as to show the head of the figure on the stretcher to a few of the audience at one side of the theatre, though neither the author nor I had any intention of allowing any portion of the supposed corpse to be visible. I am quite certain, however, that the man's 'head and shoulders' were not 'streaked with paint,' and that no attempt of any sort was made to indicate 'hideous disfigurement.'

"Yours sincerely,

"ELIZABETH ROBINS."

"*May 23rd,* 1893."

" MY DEAR ARCHER,—As the producer of *Alan's Wife,* I can unhesitatingly assure you that the 'head and shoulders' of the man who figured as the corpse on the stretcher were not 'streaked with paint to indicate some hideous disfigurement.' As it was not intended that he should be visible to the audience, I was under no temptation to commit any such hideous crudity.   "Always yours,

"H. DE LANGE."

"*May 22nd,* 1893."

Appendix II.

A Question of Priority.

To the Editor of *The Westminster Gazette.*

" SIR,—In Mr. Archer's letter to you *apropos* of a play called *Alan's Wife,* he states that the story on which that play is founded, and which describes a baptism scene as in ' Tess of the D'Urbevilles,' was published in a Swedish magazine before the English novel.

"'I learn from Mr. Archer that the actual date of the Swedish magazine was January, 1891. This bears out his printed assertion, my baptism scene having appeared in the *Fortnightly Review* about May or June of the same year.

" The coincidence being somewhat an odd one, will you allow me to say that the chapters of ' Tess ' containing this incident were in the hands of Messrs. Tillotson and Sons, the syndicate-publishers of Bolton, so early as September, 1889, and were partly put into type by their printers at that date, though (for reasons that had nothing to do with the subject of the story) I asked the firm to allow me to withdraw the MS., which they consented to do. Later on in the same year it was read by some London editors.

" Messrs. Tillotson would, I have no doubt, testify to these facts if required, as would also the London editors ; thus carrying us back to a date a year and a quarter before the publication of the Swedish tale—whatever that priority may be worth in a resemblance presumably accidental.

" Yours faithfully,
"THOMAS HARDY."

"*May* 9, 1893."

www.ingramcontent.com/pod-product-compliance
Lightning Source LLC
Chambersburg PA
CBHW030545270326
41927CB00008B/1516